Praise for Pathfinders

Whether we realized it or not, we all need a Personal Board of Advisors to help us navigate our career journeys. Pete Schramm does a terrific job of outlining the need and how to leverage your team to encourage, nurture, and support you.

Frank Wittenauer, Managing Director, People First Consulting

In a world captivated by the myth of the lone achiever, Pete offers a compelling counter-narrative: the quest for self and professional growth as a collective venture. His book is not merely a reflection of his relentless pursuit of learning and betterment, but a skillfully crafted roadmap guiding us towards a realm where seeking help is not a sign of weakness, but a testament to enlightened courage. Pete embodies every word in this book. This is a book I look forward to gifting to anyone who thinks they are capable of more.

Joe Mechlinski, NYT's and WSJ Best Selling Author, CEO of SHIFT

At the heart of sculpting our desired existence lies a powerful tool— intentionality. Pathfinders delves into this concept, offering readers a meticulously crafted roadmap for amplifying one's potential. Beyond traditional self-help advice, this book introduces a novel idea: constructing a Personal Board of Advisors. By guiding readers through this innovative approach, Pathfinders emphasizes the profound impact of curated mentorship and shared wisdom. This guide is an indispensable resource for those eager to take the reins of their life.

Tim Tannert, CEO and Founder, CultureCures

The concept of a Personal Board of Advisors is consistent with viewing ourselves as the CEOs of our own lives, a concept that can change humanity. This book is both an insightful map and fun read, and it's beneficial to professionals in virtually any state of their career in virtually any field. I thoroughly enjoyed and highly recommend this book as a true pathfinder for individuals and society at large.

Cory Warfield, Cofounder DCRBN, Upplift

Pathfinders *is a straightforward and action-orientated guide that you can use to find the next 10% of excellence in your personal and professional life regardless of if you are starting your career or a seasoned executive.*

Byron C. Wade, Healthcare Executive

Pathfinders *is a blueprint when it comes to navigating your career with the critical engagement, encouragement, guidance, and support from your Personal Board of Advisors. This book comes at such an important time given the need for organizations to more authentically address retention, and building in a laser focus on mentorship and support for the development of a Personal Board of Advisors is an important step toward career mobility and excellence.*

Geoffrey M. Roche, Director of Workforce Development,
Siemens Healthineers

In a world filled with career uncertainties, Pathfinders *equips us with the tools and wisdom to navigate our professional journeys with confidence and purpose. If I had encountered this book earlier in my career, it would have been a game-changer.*

Pathfinders *helps you navigate the often-complex landscape of professional life delving into how to create your roadmap and establish a network of knowledge from those who have paved the way before us. I wholeheartedly recommend "Pathfinders" to young professionals and recent graduates alike—it's the mentor you wish you had from the very beginning.*

Katie Fullen, Corporate People, Experience, Culture,
Communications & Change Management Leader

If you're looking to take control of your professional advancement, then this is the book for you! Pathfinders *provides individuals their own personal handbook on how to successfully navigate and advance in any type of organization. This book goes beyond the obvious importance of mentors and offers a blueprint/checklist on how to go about setting up an entire mentoring network.* Pathfinders' *revolutionary concept Personal Board of Advisors individualizes a well-known concept only thought to be applicable to large companies and organizations. The PBA + Career Map concepts force individuals to be intentional about creating a viable mentoring network, with each board member filling a specific role with an understanding that some PBA members may be long-term while others can be temporary. Although* Pathfinders *is intended to help individuals, it can also serve as a valuable tool for leaders and HR professionals looking to advise employees on how to establish a successful mentoring network or to enhance their own mentoring program. Bottom line, I wish* Pathfinders *had been available when I started my career thirty years ago.*

Colonel Dalian A. Washington Sr, US Air Force (RET)

If you want the best-in-class "how to succeed" book, this is the one you need. Pete Schramm is the go-to guy for mapping your career and your life. His tailored fit strategies are not one-size-fits-all, so if you are looking for an action-based, disciplined approach to creating your own Personal Board of Advisors, this is the book for you!

John Putzier, M.S., SPHR, President,
Redline Performance Management (RPM)

The most successful organizations of the future will be those who put their people first and create a culture of belonging. Pete Schramm has created a one-of-a-kind process that places each person in charge of their own professional career development. It will be imperative for organizations looking to empower their employees to institutionalize the Pathfinders *methodology, as it is the only way to both expand your self-awareness and be empowered through building your own Personal Board of Advisors.*

PJ Jackson, *Author of* The Labyrinth Influence:
Awaken the Wisdom Within

Embark on a purpose-driven journey with Pete Schramm's Pathfinders, a guide that doesn't merely navigate you to success but enriches every stride with intrinsic value and connection to your deeper "why." This book transcends traditional career guidance, inviting you to weave your own values, desires, and purpose into every decision, ensuring each milestone is not just achieved but deeply resonant and meaningful. Pete becomes more than a guide; he becomes a co-navigator, mentoring you to interpret, embrace, and own every twist and turn on your path, cultivating a career that's both successful and profoundly fulfilling. Pete shows you how your Personal Board of Advisors evolve into integral partners, reflecting, and championing your authentic journey towards impactful and genuine accomplishments. After reading this book, you will be empowered to traverse a path where every step of your career journey is a purposeful, enriching movement towards a career imbibed with true meaning, leadership, and heartfelt success.

Jason Weiss, President, Jason Weiss Consulting

Mentorship has been an important theme weaved throughout my professional communication courses. Now, I can recommend Pathfinders to my college students as the "how-to" guide in building and maintaining relationships that will support their professional (and personal) growth. Thank you, Pete Schramm, for creating a valuable resource that thoughtfully explains the value of a personal board of advisors.

*Tricia Pritchard, Director of Community Employment
Development and Communication Instructor,
Butler County Community College*

Pete is an electric public speaker, compelling his audiences to take ownership of their professional success by investing in themselves and those around them. I'm impressed that Pete was able to capture his energy and passion for improving the human experience at work within this book. What a great resource for anyone seeking direction on where to go next in their career—and who they should pull in to help them navigate the way.

*Dr. Victoria Mattingly, Organizational Psychologist
and CEO of Mattingly Solutions*

Pathfinders is a professional growth framework for all generations and for all stages in life. At times when the career directions are unclear, some of what so-called best practices solutions aren't as effective as before. Individuals have a case to take ownership of their paths by proactively surrounding themselves with the right village that will anticipate roadblocks and provide nothing but the best, honest and timely advice and perspective into their career journey. Pathfinders is a framework that sets the structure and rules of engagement that allows you to focus on your learning and mitigates the risk of individuals being non-strategic about professional development. It shortcuts the growth and potential realization we all have.

Livia Macedo, Global Talent Leader, Executive Coach

Since the early 19th century, organizations have used boards of directors to provide oversight and guidance. It makes so much sense to apply this best practice to an individual's career, adding diverse skills, expertise, and perspective to help the individual grow. This dynamic functions as a catalyst to promote orthogonal thinking and accelerate professional development and growth in an expedited fashion that would otherwise take decades. Pathfinders isn't just a book on my shelf, I've applied its principles to my professional career, helping me fast-track my transformation from a consultant to a successful Woman Owned Small Business owner. I am indebted to Pete for his insight and recommend this book to anyone who wants to leapfrog into their purpose.

Dr. Keisha Benson Woods, CEO of Reverse-iT Mentoring

PATHFINDERS

NAVIGATING YOUR
CAREER MAP
WITH A PERSONAL
BOARD OF ADVISORS

PETE SCHRAMM

Lattitude

This book may be purchased in bulk for business or educational use.
The Lattitude Team is also available for keynote talks aligned with concepts in this book.

For more information, contact **Pathfinders@GoLattitude.com**

To reference this research in academic work, please use the following citation:

Schramm, P. (2023). Pathfinders: Navigating your career map
with a personal board of advisors. Lattus, Inc.

FIRST EDITION
Designed by **Ian White**, www.ianpauljameswhite.com
Edited by **Allison L. Goldstein**, alg@allisonlgoldstein.com
Proofread by **Adeline Hull**, adeline@elevatededitspot.com
Coordination, planning, and graphics with
Jodi Davis Gonzales, jodi@yourjoteam.com
Marketing by **Jodi Brandstetter**, jodi@letscincy.com
Digital Strategy and SEO by **Morvan Carrier**, morvan@salesodyssey.com

ISBN: 9798865561804
Imprint: Independently published

To Mum, Dad, and my brother, Luke—Through the highs and lows of my corporate journey, the triumphs and trials in travel and sports, and the unpredictable twists of the entrepreneurial roller coaster, your unwavering love, guidance, and support have been my constant. Thank you for not only being my family but also the pillars of my Personal Board of Advisors, every step of the way.

CONTENTS

FOREWORD

In a world that often feels transactional and disconnected, Pete Schramm's book arrives as an urgently needed blueprint for those who aspire to live and lead from the heart. Pete's ability to distill decades of wisdom into a methodology for both personal and professional success is nothing short of revolutionary. To the readers embarking on this transformative journey, know that the guidebook you're holding is more than just advice—it's a manifesto for making meaningful changes in your life and the lives around you.

Pete weaves a compelling narrative that mirrors the core beliefs that have guided me throughout my diverse career paths: the essentiality of human-centered design and the irreplaceable value of experience ecosystems. From my perspective as someone who has led people and organizations in roles ranging from Chief Innovation Officer to CEO, this book offers the missing manual for the new age of heart-centered leadership, one that Peter so eloquently champions.

Pete's approach to structuring relationships is a much-needed blend of the organic and the intentional. He understands that some of life's most treasured partnerships come from the serendipity of an unexpected meeting, but he also respects the power of a well-curated mentorship. Through a career landscape that has become ever-transient, a balanced approach like Pete's is a timeless asset. The way he outlines the creation of a personal board—the central tenet of this book—serves as a navigational tool that is as versatile as it is enduring.

Pete speaks directly to the rise of career mobility as a sought-after trait in today's professional landscape. His methodology isn't bound by titles or organizational structures, but is portable, moving with you as you navigate new roles or even entire career shifts. This makes the book an essential read for professionals at various stages of their journey, from motivated graduates to seasoned executives. The universality of his insights is its greatest strength, underlining the book's core message that human connections are the bedrock upon which all successful endeavors are built.

One of the most compelling aspects of Pete's work is his emphasis on mentorship—both giving and receiving. The stories he shares serve as a testament to the symbiotic benefits of these relationships, and they resonate deeply with my own experiences. In a world where people often wonder, "Why should I invest my time in mentorship?" Pete offers powerful, evidence-based arguments that reveal how such relationships become crucibles for transformative change and unparalleled growth.

Although the methodology in this book may seem extensive, its implementation can absolutely be incremental. For those starting with a blank slate, focusing initially on the career map and the first few board seats can pave the way for a rewarding and fulfilling journey. For those further along, the guidance on refining and refreshing one's board can be immediately adopted.

Pathfinders will resonate with anyone who seeks to blend ambition with soulfulness and strategy with empathy. In the immense landscape of professional advice, this book stands out as a beacon for those who understand that success, in its truest form, is a byproduct of getting the human experience right. If you're ready to embrace that simple, challenging objective, read on. It's time to create your own team of pathfinders.

Shawn Nason, Founder and Chief Experience Officer, MOFI

INTRODUCTION

In the vast expanse of the professional world, a consistent truth emerges, much like a guiding star: relationships are the compasses that navigate us through turbulent waters and accelerate our journey in many ways. My first relationships were with my parents. Growing up with them on a farm, I learned the value of hard work and resilience from these early-stage mentors in my life. When it came to navigating the intricacies of professional occupations, I had no charted course or relationships with mentors to guide me. My journey was filled with trial and error in those early, tumultuous days.

At my first professional job, I asked my boss what could help me to be the best employee he ever had. He shared this invaluable advice:

"Find yourself a great mentor."

This advice helped set me on a quest for a mentor, even though I was unsure where to find one, what to ask them, and how to make the most of our time together.

I met Brian, my first Functional Mentor, through a class provided at work, and our professional relationship blossomed far beyond mentorship, teaching me the patience required to steer through tricky waters. Paula, who was a visionary and served as my first workplace Champion, expanded my horizons beyond the immediate coastlines, teaching me how to prepare for and anticipate the uncharted. Last, but not least, Kim served as one of my most impactful Supervisors. Her resilience against the persistent harsh tides taught me there are lessons to learn from every storm.

I learned how to excel in my current roles and was able to avoid the pitfalls that my guides had faced on their paths. My ability to develop win-win relationships expanded, and as my network grew and promotions continued, my toolbox filled with professional skills I never knew existed.

As I sailed further, I realized that one mentor, one guide, wasn't enough. The waters of professionalism were too vast, too diverse. To truly understand the depth and breadth, I needed diverse guides—individuals with varied experiences and perspectives. It's here that the concept of a "Personal Board of Advisors" began to take shape in my mind.

The moment of clarity, my true "aha" moment, came during the preparation for my first TEDx talk. Don't just take my word for it; *Harvard Business Review, Fortune, MIT Sloan Management Review*, and CNBC, among others, all emphasize the indispensable role of a personal advisory board. Literary greats like Napoleon Hill and contemporary figures like Reid Hoffman have also underscored its significance. But where's the blueprint? Where's the actionable path that translates these insights into practical steps? As I delved deep into the subject, Dorie Clark's work stood out, echoing the thoughts I'd been piecing together. The idea of a Personal Board of Advisors (PBA) solidified. This wasn't about just finding mentors; it was about gathering a diverse crew to navigate the vastness of the professional sea.

Drawing from my unique journey from the farm to the basketball court and around the globe (twice), from building robots for the army to starting my own company, and from lessons learned from dozens of people who've helped me, this book was crafted. It was fueled by thousands of conversations with individuals from all walks of life and thirty-nine notebooks of insights and perspectives that I recorded along the way. Think of it as a nautical chart for professionals, detailing not just the significance of a PBA but also a clear path to assembling one.

The professional voyage can be as unpredictable as the sea itself, but with a seasoned crew and a comprehensive map, any destination becomes reachable. Let this book be both your map and guide to assembling that crew and mapping out your journey. This isn't just about the "why"; it's predominantly about the "how."

You might wonder: Why invest time in this book? What's in it for you? This isn't just a recollection of my life; it's a guide to navigating your own journey. By sharing my experiences, the mistakes made, the lessons learned, and the insights gained, these chapters aim to light your path and save you time so that you do not have to repeat as many wrong turns and dead ends as I experienced over the past decade and a half of my professional journey. The purpose of this book is to help save you a few months, years, or even decades of trial and error on your professional path.

As you anchor yourself on the shores of potential with uncharted waters ahead, remember: the journey becomes not only navigable but also enriching with the right crew and compass. Unfurl your sails, trust in your compass, and allow this book to guide you toward reaching your professional North Star.

Where Are We Heading?

As we embark on the intricate voyage of our professional lives, the horizon is dotted with multiple potential destinations, each representing a dream, an aspiration, or a potential future. Every intrepid traveler understands the importance of preparation before a journey. We rely heavily on technology for guidance—a quick map search here, GPS directions there—with "re-routing, re-routing" in the GPS voice of your choosing often serving as a common soundtrack to your journeys. But what happens when technology falters, the battery drains, or we find ourselves in a place with no signal? In such moments, the weight and significance of preparation, human connection, and trusted advisors around us come to the forefront.

Embarking on the Professional Voyage

Reflect on one of your most memorable journeys. Was it the map that made it special, or was it the local guide who shared hidden gems, advised against certain routes, and introduced you to experiences you hadn't even imagined? Our professional journey, much like a grand expedition, teems with multiple tantalizing destinations. Each beckons with its unique allure: leadership roles, specialization, or the high seas of entrepreneurship. While the digital age has equipped us with an array of tools to guide our way, the question remains: Can technology alone truly steer us through the nuances, challenges, and choices that define our careers? In my experience, "merely sprinkling on some tech" does not solve most problems.

The Invaluable Human Touch in Navigation

Even the most advanced GPS can't introduce you to a hidden gem of a café or warn you about the local bridge that's recently become impassable. This is where the wisdom of the locals becomes invaluable. In our professional journey, this guiding force is your PBA. They don't just indicate the way; they enrich your path with personal insights, foresight, and stories that add depth to your experience.

In a world where we are so intertwined with technology, there's an undeniable comfort in knowing that there are individuals—human pathfinders—ready to guide, challenge, and support you, especially when technology lets you down or can't provide the depth of guidance you seek.

Our "Pathfinders"

The title of this book, *Pathfinders: Navigating Your Career Map with a Personal Board of Advisors*, is inspired in part by the US Army's Pathfinders. These elite soldiers don't just chart the course; they ensure the journey is safe, strategic, and informed. Similarly, your PBA is your squadron of elite guides, ensuring you're not just moving, but moving with purpose, clarity, and wisdom.

Our endeavor goes beyond merely plotting a trajectory on a career map. I aim to introduce you to the profound impact of having human navigators—individuals whose experiences, expertise, and insights can transform your professional voyage. As we venture deeper, you'll learn how to craft your career map and identify, engage, and cultivate these human pathfinders.

Army Pathfinders are trained to provide navigational aid and advisory services to military aircraft in areas designated by supported unit commanders. The Pathfinders' secondary missions include providing advice and limited aid to units planning air assault or airdrop operations.

Remember, while tools and technology are instrumental, genuine enrichment comes from the human touch, the wisdom of those who've journeyed before you. After all, isn't every voyage better with trusted companions by your side? Let's set forth on this enlightening journey together, harnessing both modern tools and timeless wisdom.

Figure 1: Comparing the process and approach to a trip we take in life (outside of work) to a process we can use to approach our own professional development journey.

The Concept of Advisory Boards

Just as companies lean on boards for strategic guidance and accountability, you can adopt a similar strategy for personal growth. But first, what exactly is an advisory board?

Companies often have two main guiding bodies: a board of directors and a board of advisors. While their functions might seem similar, they cater to distinct aspects of a business. The board of directors primarily oversees governance, making critical decisions and ensuring the company's health and growth. On the other hand, a board of advisors offers expertise and advice, often without authoritative powers, to help the company navigate challenges and opportunities.

Picture this: a personally tailored team of mentors, enthusiasts, and specialists committed to your growth and success. This is your PBA. It's a group you curate, consisting of trusted individuals offering a variety of perspectives, vital advice, and unwavering encouragement. They are your mentors, your inspiration, your go-tos for clarity amidst confusion. It's about surrounding yourself with a circle that believes in your potential and is eager to see you realize it.

Welcome to *Pathfinders: Navigating Your Career Map with a Personal Board of Advisors.*

In this book, we'll delve deep into the tenets, strategies, and actionable steps to curate your PBA and plot your career trajectory. Whether you're kickstarting your career journey, aspiring to leadership, or aiming for further personal growth, *Pathfinders* is tailored to arm you with knowledge, tools, and motivation to wade through the intricacies of personal and professional growth.

Figure 2: Visual representation of the eight seats on your PBA. Although there are ten roles to choose from, I suggest only having eight members on your board at a time. We will discuss which roles are more valuable at various stages of your professional journey as the book continues!

What You Will Find in This Book

Throughout these pages, you will discover a wealth of insights, real-life use cases, and actionable steps and strategies that have been proven to accelerate personal and professional growth. You'll gain an understanding of the roles and responsibilities of PBA members, how to identify the right individuals to fill those roles, and how to establish clear goals and expectations for each member. We will go over the art of effective communication, maintaining healthy board dynamics, and nurturing long-term relationships that foster growth and success.

Sounds like a lot of work, huh? You are already extremely busy—how can you possibly have time to learn how to do this and then track it as well? To ease your load, we will also explore how technology and digital platforms can enhance your board experience, allowing for seamless collaboration and access to resources. We'll discuss the significance of cultural sensitivity and inclusivity in board dynamics, as well as the importance of self-care, well-being, and continuous learning in sustaining long-term success.

This book goes beyond theory; it's a practical guide that encourages action at every step. Inside you'll find exercises, templates, and tools that enable you to implement the concepts discussed and track your progress effectively. Additionally, it integrates with our companion website, serving as a valuable resource for managing and tracking your personal board over time and providing a seamless experience for your growth journey.

Your Guide to Icons Used in This Book

As we go through this book, you will find icons that guide you in a few directions. I used these to break up the text and call your attention to key points, emphasize a point, or push you toward an action!

 Self Reflection

 Idea or Fun Fact/Stat

 Pete's Perspective/Story

 Take Action!

 Refers to Another Part of the Book

 External Resource

 Opportunity to use the Companion Website

 Caution! What to Avoid

Figure 3: Outlines the icons used throughout the book to call your attention to specific concepts or guide you to take action. You saw a light bulb earlier calling out a fun fact about Pathfinders.

The QR code below will take you to the companion website to begin tracking your journey. After doing more than fifty workshops on this topic and handing out hundreds of pages of worksheets, I realized that we needed a more fluid solution. Tech helps us make the experience truly our own. Scan the code with your phone or type in the URL below the code to get started.

Figure 4: QR code that will link you to the companion website as you continue through the book. The URL to type into your computer (if you do not want to scan from a mobile device) is **https://www.pathfinders.golattitude.com/book** *This QR code is also on the back cover of the book.*

As we continue through the book, you will also see a gear-in-hand image reminding you when it's a good time to pop back into the website and take action!

So, are you ready to unlock the immense potential of your PBA? Are you prepared to embrace a network of mentors, supporters, and experts who will propel you toward success? If your answer is a resounding "yes," then this book is your roadmap. Let's embark together on this transformative journey of building your PBA and accelerating your professional growth beyond what you ever thought possible.

How to Get the Most Out of This Book

The true value of this book lies not just in reading it but in moving beyond the hypothetical and actively applying the principles and strategies outlined within. If you have the opportunity to fully immerse yourself in this book, embrace the journey with enthusiasm, curiosity, and a commitment to growth. Dive into the material, engage in self-reflection, and take intentional action to build your PBA. This is not merely a task to add to your busy lifestyle, but a path toward meaningful professional development. By dedicating focused effort and applying the principles and strategies outlined within, you will unlock the true value of this book and invest in your growth, reaping rewards that extend beyond superficial tips. Professional development does take time, and when we do it with intention, it pays off, but this is not a "quick fix" solution where you can simply "sprinkle on some tips" and then do nothing.

Before you dive into the pages, it's essential to prepare yourself for the transformative journey ahead. This section will provide you with valuable insights and tips on how to make the most of your reading experience, maximize your learning, and apply the concepts effectively. By following these guidelines, you will embark on a purposeful and enriching exploration of building your PBA.

Cultivate a Growth Mindset: Approach this book with an open and growth-oriented mindset. Embrace the idea that personal and professional development is a lifelong journey and be willing to challenge your existing beliefs and perspectives. Adopt a mindset that views obstacles as opportunities for growth and learning.

Carol Dweck's work and her book *Mindset: The New Psychology of Success* on the growth mindset emphasizes the belief that intelligence and abilities can be developed through effort, persistence, and a positive attitude toward challenges. Embracing this mindset in professional development can lead to resilience and success, allowing individuals to thrive during challenging times, learn from setbacks, and foster a cooperative environment that values the growth and effort of everyone involved.

Pursue Action-Oriented Learning: Challenge yourself to put the concepts in this book into practice and apply them in real-life scenarios. This approach will translate knowledge into tangible results. To amplify your learning and implementation, integrate the concepts from the book with the referenced workshops, resources, and companion website. The website will serve as a valuable tool for ongoing support and reflection as you continue building out your career map. Change can be difficult and take some time. We are going on this journey together!

Set Clear Intentions and Goals: Take a moment to reflect on your motivations and intentions for reading this book. What specific goals or aspirations do you have for building a PBA? Write them down and keep them in mind as you progress through each chapter. Having clear intentions will help you stay focused and derive maximum value from the content.

Take Notes, Journal, and Self-Reflect: Keep a notebook or journal handy while reading. (If you want to take things to the next level, use some of the technology we suggest as you go through the book!) Jot down key concepts, insights, and personal reflections that resonate with you. Highlight passages, underline important ideas, and make annotations to facilitate future reference. We also provide space at the end of each chapter for reflection and "aha moments."

Seek Support and Accountability: Building a PBA is a journey that can be enhanced with support and accountability. Consider forming a study group or reading circle with peers who are also interested in personal development. Schedule regular discussions to share insights, discuss challenges, and hold each other accountable for taking action.

To amplify your learning and implementation, integrate the concepts from the book with the referenced workshops, resources, and companion website. The website will serve as a valuable tool for ongoing support and reflection as you continue building out your career map.

Now, let's embark on this transformative journey together and unleash the power of your personal board for accelerated professional growth and fulfillment.

BUILDING YOUR PERSONAL BOARD OF ADVISORS

Part I of this book sets the stage for how to build your Personal Board of Advisors (PBA) and introduces the ten board seats to think about on your journey. We will also dig into the concept of a career map that can be used as a helpful guide or career compass in each of the growth conversations with board members. Part II of the book will delve into engaging with the specific board members, and Part III wraps up with how to manage your board over time to maximize results.

CHAPTER 1

UNLOCKING YOUR POTENTIAL WITH A PERSONAL BOARD OF ADVISORS

"If you want to go fast, go alone.
If you want to go far, go together."

African Proverb

We kick off this book by highlighting the importance of embarking on your journey with the right people who will guide you toward the right destination for the right reasons. This chapter outlines ten personal board seats that can be filled and introduces each of the advisor roles. Upon completion, you will also understand at which stages of professional growth the board can add the most value!

Collaborative Voyagers and Solo Explorers Picture two professionals embarking on their respective career voyages. Their end destinations are similar in that they want to achieve success in the business world with a fulfilling career they enjoy. Yet, the routes they chart and the choices they make lead them on incredibly distinct paths, directly influenced by their perspectives on collaborative growth and the guides they choose—or neglect—to have by their side.

First, let's set our sights on Jamie. Working alongside Jamie in corporate America, I had a front-row seat to the solitary sailor's saga. Filled with ambition, Jamie believed they could intuitively read the winds and tides. Setting sail alone on the tumultuous sea of career aspirations, Jamie found themself frequently battling unexpected tempests and veering off course, with each job pulling them further from their true north. Their vessel, while resilient, often faced choppy waters, and the horizon was consistently clouded by unforeseen squalls. Fleeting successes were found, and some destinations were reached, but I still see Jamie going alone, no longer going fast, and not yet at their desired career destination.

Then, on the horizon, there's Joe, with whom I also worked. Joe's approach was starkly different. Recognizing early on the invaluable lessons even stormy seas could impart, he adopted the mantra that tempests craft the finest sailors. He also knew that wisdom from experienced navigators could mean the difference between aimless drifting and a purpose-driven voyage. Assembling a dedicated PBA, he found his guiding lighthouses and used their insights to steer him clear of treacherous shoals and direct him smoothly through the most daunting waves. The result? A journey brimming with purpose, allowing Joe to reach his professional aspirations with a mix of grace and astounding speed. I think Joe will be leading Jamie soon.

Echoing the age-old wisdom of the African proverb, "If you want to go fast, go alone. If you want to go far, go together," our careers mirror intricate voyages, made richer and clearer by the stars and lighthouses we trust to guide us.

Envision reaching your destination not just swiftly, but with tales of exhilarating navigation rather than stories of harrowing detours. Imagine mastering the unpredictable currents of the corporate world, leveraging both challenges and mentors to shape your success. The thrill of such a journey awaits you, and it begins with assembling your very own guiding constellation.

Candid Compasses Beyond Familiar Shores

Imagine setting sail on the vast ocean with just your map and a crew you've picked based on fondness. Now, this crew, being your friends and family, are steadfast in their love for you. They'd do anything to keep you happy, to see a smile on your face. However, in doing so, they might sometimes keep quiet when they see dark clouds forming ahead, for fear of causing you anxiety or despair. Their primary role, after all, is to be your emotional support, keeping you stable and buoyant.

Enter the lighthouse keepers—or, in our context, your PBA. These are individuals chosen not just for the comfort they bring but for their sharp eyes, experience reading the sea, and ability to discern upcoming tempests even when the skies seem clear.

For instance, consider Jessica, an enthusiastic professional who was set on charting a new venture. Friends and family cheered her on, fearing that any critique might dampen her spirit. However, when she presented the idea to her PBA, one of them, a seasoned entrepreneur, raised concerns about a potential competitor's edge. The critique wasn't meant to discourage but to fortify her strategy, a move that eventually helped her navigate her venture successfully.

These advisors aren't just there for their strategic prowess but for their unyielding commitment to your growth. If your ship seems to veer off course, they are the ones to gently, yet firmly, redirect your compass, ensuring you're aligned with your true north. They will ask probing questions like "Have you considered the implications of this decision?" or "Remember your ultimate goal; does this path lead toward it?"

The brilliance of a PBA lies in its members' vantage points. Positioned at different parts of your journey, they can anticipate challenges, see further than you might be able to at the moment, and have the courage to voice concerns because you've built a relationship anchored in mutual respect and a shared mission: your success and growth.

Your advisors hold you accountable, always urging you to understand your motivations. In a world filled with yes-men, they are the brave souls who, with unwavering support, ask "why" and challenge you to be the best version of yourself. As your vessel sails ahead, these guiding lighthouses ensure you're not just riding the waves but mastering them, setting you on a course toward clear skies and your desired haven.

Personal board seats covered in this book are:

1. Buddy: The Peer Support Advisor
2. Accountability Partner: The Commitment Enforcer and Responsibility Advisor
3. Functional Mentor: The Experienced Guide and Inside Advisor
4. Cross-Functional Mentor: The Specialist Mentor and Outside Advisor
5. Coach: The Project-Based Tactical Advisor
6. Sponsor: The Influential Advocate and Superconnector Advisor
7. Champion: The Strategic Guide and "Split-Level" Advisor
8. Ally: The Collaborative Partner and Perspective Advisor
9. Manager/Supervisor: Your Boss and Daily Advisor
10. Successor: The Protégé-in-Training and Reverse Mentor

The icons below represent each of the ten seats that we will describe throughout the book. You will mostly see these in Part II, as we manage our personal board and turn the concept into a reality!

 **Buddy**
The Peer Support Advisor

 Sponsor
The Influential Advocate and Superconnector Advisor

 Accountability Partner
The Responsibility Advisor

 Champion
The Strategic Guidance and Support Advisor "split level"

 Functional Mentor
The Experienced Guide and Inside Advisor

 Ally
The Collaborative Supporting Partner and Perspective Advisor

 Cross-Functional Mentor
The Specialist Mentor and Outside Advisor

 Supervisor/Manager
Your Bosss and Tactical Advisor

 Coach
The Project-Baased Tactical Advisor (Various Flavors)

 Successor
Protege-in-Training and Reverse Mentor

Figure 5: The ten board seats that we will discuss throughout this book.

Charting Your Course

Imagine setting sail without a clear destination in mind or recognizing the unique capabilities of your ship. No matter how sturdy the vessel or favorable the winds, without understanding where you're going or the ship's strengths and weaknesses, you'd be constantly battling the currents and often losing direction. Similarly, in our professional voyage, many of us set sail without truly recognizing and leveraging our strengths or being mindful of our weaknesses. We drift for years, sometimes decades, in jobs that don't resonate with our passions, barely skimming the surface of what we can truly achieve. If you are OK with the exploratory, drifting approach to your career, then a PBA is probably not the tool to help you on your adventure.

Your advisors are seasoned navigators who've weathered many storms and understand the importance of playing to one's strengths and creating compensating controls for weaknesses. They don't just offer counsel; they challenge you, pushing you to self-reflect and pinpoint your core competencies. With their insights, you can bolster career mobility, making informed choices that align with your passions and strengths.

It's not uncommon for professionals to take an agonizingly long time to discern their strengths, let alone confront their weaknesses. We often fall into the trap of conforming to the "safe" choices or paths that seem promising to the majority. While these may offer immediate rewards, they often lead to stagnation, unfulfilled aspirations, and a lingering sense of "what if?" This is where having a dynamic career map, tailored to your strengths, becomes paramount.

The concept of career mapping isn't about etching a static plan but adopting an agile approach. As the world of work changes, so do our roles, interests, and the skills we need to thrive. To be truly agile is to have the capacity to pivot, to adapt, and to move with intent. Your career map is not a one-size-fits-all but a living document, changing as you evolve, much like agile methodologies employed in successful businesses today.

Your PBA serves as a strategic think tank, aiding you in interpreting the ever-changing job landscape and positioning yourself effectively. By viewing your career as an agile journey, you remain receptive to shifts, always ready to leverage new opportunities. Together with the counsel of your board, you're not just passively sailing; you're navigating with purpose, armed with a deep understanding of your strengths and the agility to capitalize on them.

With this methodology, you're not just on a voyage; you're on an expedition, purposefully moving toward horizons that resonate with your strengths and dreams.

Career mobility refers to the ability to move and advance within or between roles and organizations throughout one's professional journey, encompassing both vertical (promotions) and horizontal (changing roles or departments) progression. It's not always just up, up, up like a ladder.

When to Build Your Personal Board

The journey to success is rarely a solo endeavor. It's often an accrued collective effort, a symphony of voices that guide, support, and inspire us along the way. This is where the concept of a PBA comes into play. But when should you start building this board? The answer is simple: as soon as possible. The importance of networking before you need to leverage your network cannot be overstated. If you wait until you need other people, you risk being perceived as opportunistic. However, if you've already demonstrated your value and willingness to help others, you'll have accrued the trust of your network, making them more likely to recognize your value and come to your aid.

I learned that a proactive approach was significantly more successful than a reactive one when preparing to transition into a job at the end of my rotational development program. After hours of research and exploration, I reached out to people who had previously filled each of the positions I was considering, asking what each of the four opportunities would entail and how I might fit into each. It was all about me, me, me, and I wasn't necessarily seeking first to understand more about their background and professional journey. None of these people truly knew what was best for my long-term development—they'd just met me!—so thank goodness they spent a few moments talking with me when I reached out. This is when I realized that a core group of advisors was necessary before big decision points arrived.

This is a great time to visit the companion website to start reviewing some of your career planning assets. More details can be found in the Appendix: Companion Website Resources, regarding how to do this. Remember how I mentioned that the goal of this book is to make your life easier, save you time, and help you grow? The career companion tools will help you track details, actions, and progress as we move through this book together.

Early Career Advantages

Starting your career can feel like navigating uncharted waters. There are crucial decisions to make, paths to choose, and challenges to overcome. Building a PBA early in your career can provide guidance during these pivotal moments. These advisors can offer insights from their own experiences, helping you avoid common pitfalls and capitalize on opportunities you might not have recognized on your own. Moreover, cultivating a supportive network from the start can provide a solid foundation for mapping out your professional journey, fostering relationships that can evolve and grow as you do.

Career Transition and Growth

As your career progresses, you may find yourself facing new challenges such as job changes, promotions, or shifts in your professional focus. During these transitions, your PBA can provide invaluable guidance and support. The advisors can offer objective advice, help you weigh your options, and provide reassurance during uncertain times. Furthermore, your board can facilitate continuous growth and development, helping you refine your skills, expand your knowledge, and stay abreast of industry trends.

Professional Plateau

If you're feeling stuck on a professional plateau, this book can provide fresh perspectives, strategies, and a network of advisors to help reignite your growth trajectory. Sometimes, we get so caught up in our day-to-day work and life that we forget to step back and take time for some "self-strategery" (a fun word I like to use for "strategic thinking"). While writing this book, I interviewed more than one hundred professionals in their late twenties, thirties, and forties. In our quick chats, they had their own "aha moments" and began to build out their boards again. Most of them had identified a few seats already filled (but not yet formalized) before we dropped from our call or finished our last sip of coffee!

Entrepreneurship and Innovation "Outside Corporate"

For those who venture into entrepreneurship or innovation outside the corporate world, a PBA can be particularly beneficial. This board can provide diverse perspectives, industry insights, and strategic guidance, all of which are crucial for navigating the dynamic and often unpredictable landscape of entrepreneurship. They can challenge your ideas, push your boundaries, and encourage you to think outside the box. These advisors not only provide guidance but also serve as a source of inspiration and motivation.

Action and Reflection

As we wrap up Chapter 1, start to think about what you can be doing today and what you are maybe already doing but just not tracking (yet!).

1. What specific goals or aspirations do you have for building a PBA?

2. How can a PBA help you at the current stage of your career?

3. Jot down key concepts, aha moments, insights, and personal reflections that arose in your mind as you read this chapter.

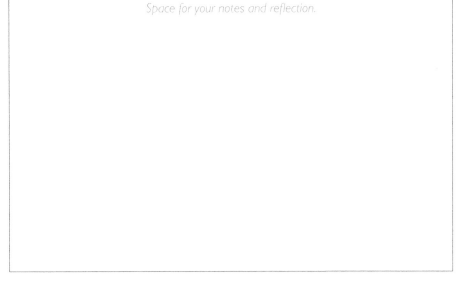

Space for your notes and reflection.

CHAPTER 2

ORCHESTRATING STRATEGIC GROWTH AND NURTURING ACCOUNTABILITY

*"Plans fail for lack of counsel, but with
many advisers, they succeed."*

Proverbs 15:22

As we embark on this chapter, we're poised to uncover a transformative concept that has steered multibillion-dollar corporations to success and, when mismanaged, has also led to their downfall. First, we will grasp the historical depth and diverse roots of advisory boards, understanding how they've evolved across cultures and eras. Next, we'll draw parallels between these corporate entities and our own professional journey, learning how the principles of strategic planning, accountability, and risk management can be reimagined for personal growth. Finally, through compelling real-world examples, we'll cover both cautionary tales and inspiring success stories, offering invaluable lessons on the significance of adaptability, foresight, and trusted mentorship. As you delve into these insights, this chapter promises to arm you with actionable strategies to not only navigate your career but to truly shape it.

Historical Tapestry of Guidance

Corporate boards, historically known for strategic oversight and accountability in the business realm, have roots that go much deeper and span diverse global traditions. However, these structures have occasionally been associated with Western-centric capitalism and oppressive imperialism. As we unveil the concept of personal boards, we derive inspiration and insight from these rich, global traditions to weave a new narrative of personal growth and strategic direction.

The Mauryan Empire in ancient India convened a council of ministers to provide strategic advice to the emperor, reflecting the ancient governance structures that predated modern corporate entities. Similarly, the Arochukwu kingdom in present-day Nigeria with the Ibini Ukpabi is another testament to the early forms of advisory boards. These foundational structures influenced the rise of modern corporate boards, with entities like the Dutch East India Company in 1602 and the British East India Company in the seventeenth century pioneering the framework.[1,2] By the nineteenth century, the establishment of the New York Stock Exchange led to the formation of corporate boards in the United States, further shaping the modern corporate landscape.[3]

Facets of Corporate Boards

A board of advisors and a board of directors may sound similar, but they have different remits.

Board of Advisors: Primarily focus on imparting expertise, mentoring, and providing insights from their extensive industry knowledge. Their independent perspectives often breathe fresh life into a company's strategic vision.

Board of Directors: Govern the company's strategic direction, ensure legal compliance, oversee top executives, and represent the interests of shareholders.

Although these boards have distinct roles, they are both intended to help the company achieve strategic success. Their continuous engagement with management through annual reports, financial statements, and updates ensures informed decision-making that aligns with the company's future vision. Figure 6 shows how a corporate board of directors is responsible for guiding the leader charged with steering the company itself. The board does not typically get involved with all the work being done, instead, it sticks to background activities of strategic guidance and accountability.

---

1   Gelderblom, O. 2013. *Cities of Commerce: The Institutional Foundations of International Trade in the Low Countries, 1250–1650.* Princeton University Press.

2   Robins, N. 2006. *The Corporation that Changed the World: How the East India Company Shaped the Modern Multinational.* Pluto Press.

3   Wright, R. E. 2015. *Corporation Nation: The Rise of the Modern Corporation and the Making of the American Economy.* The University of Pennsylvania Press.

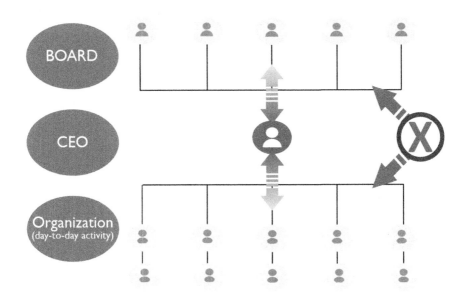

Figure 6: A corporate board of directors or advisors guides the CEO but does not get involved in the day-to-day activities of the organization.

Your Career, Your Corporation: Translating Board Principles to Personal Growth

Consider yourself as your own enterprise. If corporate boards shape the destiny of multibillion-dollar companies and truly have the company's best interests at heart, imagine what a PBA could do for an individual with people who take an interest in you! It's about drawing parallels and transforming corporate principles of strategic planning, accountability, and risk management into personal growth trajectories. Your board is a fusion of mentors, sponsors, coaches, and perhaps a few well-wishers. Their collective wisdom is the catalyst driving your personal growth and career evolution.

Note: As we navigate this journey, it's imperative to address potential conflicts of interest and power dynamics. A more in-depth exploration of potential conflicts will be addressed in Part III.

The Tales of Three Boards: Lessons and Warnings

Understanding corporate boards can shed light on how their principles might be applied to personal boards. Drawing inspiration from both positive and negative board examples, one can glean invaluable lessons that can be implemented in personal career strategies.

Enron: A Cautionary Tale of Board Failure

The 2001 collapse of Enron is often cited as one of the most significant corporate failures due to a lack of board oversight. Enron's board, lauded for its independence, sadly missed or overlooked numerous internal issues, including financial irregularities and unethical practices. Their lack of due diligence and passive approach has become a textbook example of the consequences of board neglect.[4]

Blackberry: Rise, Dominance, and Decline

Blackberry's tale is one of early dominance followed by rapid decline in the mid-2010s. Once a leader in the smartphone market, Blackberry became complacent, failing to innovate or adapt to the evolving landscape. Their board, despite witnessing the rise of competitors like Apple and Android, failed to push for essential innovations or strategic shifts. This oversight eventually led to a considerable loss in market share.[5]

IBM: A Testament to Strategic Revival

IBM's revival in the 1990s remains one of the business world's most celebrated turnarounds. The company was on the brink of bankruptcy before its board made a series of strategic decisions that pivoted its direction. Their decision to bring in an outsider, Louis Vincent Gerstner Jr., as CEO, marked the start of IBM's transformation. The board's ability to recognize the need for change, adapt, and oversee a dynamic strategy is a testament to their strength and vision. This example illustrates the significance of having a board that possesses foresight, adaptability, and the courage to make tough decisions.[6]

The Danger of Misguided Mentorship

Just as corporate boards can influence the trajectory of a company, personal board members such as mentors and advisors can significantly impact an individual's career path—and not always for the better. I experienced this from a boss who sought to mold me in their image: following the same career path, working with the same people, and only focusing on a few kinds of projects, thus excluding many potential connections and interesting opportunities.

---

4   McLean, B. and P. Elkind. 2004. *The Smartest Guys in the Room: The Amazing Rise and Scandalous Fall of Enron*. Portfolio Trade.

5   McNish, J. and S. Silcoff. 2015. *Losing the Signal: The Untold Story Behind the Extraordinary Rise and Spectacular Fall of Blackberry*. Flatiron Books.

6   Gerstner, Louis V. *Who Says Elephants Can't Dance? Inside IBM's Historic Turnaround*. HarperBusiness, 2002.

Another leader-turned-mentor tried to manipulate my work to cover up a mistake that had been made. Without the outside counsel of my personal board, I might have followed through, trusting someone in a position of power whom I thought had my best interests at heart. The power of diverse perspectives and outside insight came to my rescue here. If they hadn't, I likely would have been fired for my actions.

Action and Reflection

As we wrap up Chapter 2, start to think about . . .

1. What might you add to the "bylaws" of your board for things that need to be considered in each relationship and reviewed in each conversation to proactively limit the issues from popping up?

2. When did you last review your initially agreed-upon goals and expectations with a mentor (or mentee) in one of your conversations? Are you still headed in the right direction and doing it the right way?

3. Have you stepped back to identify who the board members are for your company? (Perhaps they could fill a seat on your personal board one day!)

4. If you are going to fail, fail quickly, learn from it, and move on. We learn a lot from failing.

"Take chances, make mistakes, get messy!"

Ms. Frizzle, a character from one of my favorite childhood shows, The Magic School Bus

Space for your notes and reflection.

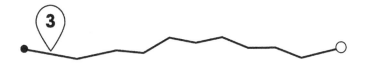

CHAPTER 3:

THE POWER OF MULTIPLE MEMBERS IN YOUR SUPPORT SYSTEM(S)

*"Surround yourself with the dreamers and the doers,
the believers and thinkers, but most of all, surround
yourself with those who see greatness within you,
even when you don't see it yourself."*

Edmund Lee, author and speaker

Edmund Lee may not be as prominent of an author or speaker as Jay Shetty, Simon Sinek, or Tony Robbins, but his quote truly encapsulates a multifaceted support system. By invoking dreamers, doers, believers, and thinkers, Lee underscores the diverse array of personalities and perspectives that can enrich an individual's personal and professional journey. These figures represent the broad spectrum of mentors one might seek: those who inspire with their visionary ideas, those who act and motivate through their achievements, those who believe unconditionally in your potential, and those who challenge and refine your thought processes. Most poignantly, the quote highlights the mentors who recognize and nurture latent potential, acting as a mirror to reflect the greatness within, especially during moments of self-doubt.

This chapter delves into the significance of diverse perspectives, emphasizing the need for a variety of insights in your PBA. We will also discuss certain traits to evaluate when determining whether an individual is a suitable candidate for your board or not the right match. Similar to sales, it's preferable to reach a "no" quickly if that's the appropriate response at the moment!

I leaned on multiple mentors when I set out to start my first tech company in 2018. I made calls to peers who filled the Buddy board seat, grabbed coffee and drinks with other mentors and accountability partners in the DC area, and then I asked a few to join me in Chicago in person for the build of our first website. A Supervisor flew out, a Mentor drove five hours, an Accountability Partner traveled from California to Chicago, and a friend let us use his apartment as our conference room! Our long weekend together was far from butterflies and rainbows—they challenged me at every turn, ensured I left no stone unturned, and helped me eliminate any possibility of ambiguity when communicating with prospective clients. Their experiences, from Wall Street consulting and investment banking to cowboy boots, fighter jets, industrial tools, and space telecommunications, brought diverse perspectives to our conversation and set me off on the right foot with my company.

Leaders with Advisory Teams

From influential leaders of the past to modern-day visionaries, the power of multiple mentors has been a common thread among those who have reached extraordinary heights. Think of iconic figures like Leonardo da Vinci who surrounded himself with experts in various fields, or the legendary investor Warren Buffett, known for seeking guidance from a select group of trusted advisors.[7,8] Their ability to assemble advisory teams demonstrates the profound impact that multiple perspectives and expertise can have on personal growth and achievement.

Mentorship Mosaic: The Strength in Diverse Perspectives

Diverse perspectives are crucial in personal development and decision-making. Having people who differ from you in your support system can provide a range of viewpoints and insights. Each member can contribute unique skills, experiences, and expertise to your personal growth journey. Emotional support from various individuals can offer different forms of encouragement, empathy, and motivation.

---

7   Isaacson, W. 2017. *Leonardo da Vinci*. Simon & Schuster.

8   Schroeder, A. 2008. *The Snowball: Warren Buffett and the Business of Life*. Bantam Books.

Diversity, particularly in the context of corporate America, is a multifaceted concept that encompasses a broad range of characteristics and experiences. Research has consistently found that the more diverse a corporate board is, the more financially profitable it is compared to boards that lack gender and ethnic diversity.[9] Let's continue building on the parallels between the benefits of boards leading corporations and how our personal board can help lead us. When done right, diversity is a game-changer in both contexts! Here are two definitions of diversity to help you contemplate this concept:

According to the U.S. Department of Housing and Urban Development, diversity is defined as *"the practice of including the many communities, identities, races, ethnicities, backgrounds, abilities, cultures, and beliefs of the American people, including underserved communities."*[10]

A Diligent Corporation report describes corporate diversity as *"when organizations intentionally employ a workforce of employees of varying characteristics. For instance, these characteristics could include sexual orientation, gender, race, ethnicity, religion, age, physical abilities, political ideologies, or socioeconomic status."*[11]

In simple terms, diversity is about recognizing and valuing the unique experiences, perspectives, and identities that individuals bring to the table. It's about ensuring that everyone, regardless of their background, has an equal opportunity to contribute and succeed. This challenge requires us to confront biases, break down barriers, and create inclusive environments—spaces where individuals from all identity groups feel valued, respected, seen, and heard. However, it's also an opportunity because diverse teams are more innovative, productive, and better equipped to understand and serve diverse customer bases.[12]

While working on a long shot "tough to win" proposal, I had a spontaneous idea to buy lunch for part of my team, including two of my personal board members who were collaborating with me at the time. Among the dozen of us, we spanned every generation in the workforce, from interns to executives. We had representation across technical and nontechnical functions, including engineers, lawyers, and designers, and encompassed multiple genders, races, and upbringings, with varying degrees of understanding about what a proposal actually entailed. While enjoying delightful tacos, we engaged in conversations about the task at hand.

9 Hunt, V., et al. 2018. "Delivering Through Diversity." McKinsey & Company.

10 U.S. Department of Housing and Urban Development. 2016. "HUD's Diversity and Inclusion Strategic Plan." HUD.gov.

11 Website: Diligent Corporation. "Corporate Diversity." Accessed July 5, 2023. URL: https://www.diligent.com/resources/blog/corporate-diversity.

12 Rock, D. and Grant, H. 2016. "Why Diverse Teams Are Smarter." *Harvard Business Review.*

Over the next two or so hours, we uncovered new tactics, win themes, and proposal strategies that seemed straightforward but might never have emerged without the freedom to speak openly, build on each other's ideas, and let our differences unite us. We won the proposal and secured multiple follow-on efforts with that team—and yes, we indulged in many more tacos at that same restaurant!

As we explore the concept of diversity in this book, it's crucial to emphasize that our aim is to offer a guide applicable to everyone, regardless of background. The practical ideas presented are designed to be adapted to best fit your individual needs and circumstances. There is no definitive formula for how much diversity should exist on your personal board; if there were, it would depend on you, your background, and your goals. Only you can determine when your board's diversity feels right, and even then, it's an ever-shifting target. We hold the conviction that everyone has valuable insights to offer and deserves the chance to realize their fullest potential.

In the spirit of transparency and accountability, I encourage you to examine your own biases and behaviors, both online and offline. As the saying goes, "the standard you walk past (or ignore) is the standard you accept."[13] So, if there's anything in your life that doesn't align with the values of respect, inclusivity, and fairness, now is the time to address it.

In Part III, we will delve deeper into the topic of diversity, exploring its many dimensions and providing practical strategies for fostering a diverse and inclusive PBA.

Board Prospect Preparation Checklist

When you start to outline your personal board, there are a few things to think about when evaluating and assessing each board seat to fill. We're going to review these elements in a checklist. I am not saying that you have to make a checklist like this for every single person on your prospect list, and it's not the end of the world if each board prospect does not meet every one of these criteria. However, it is worth referencing every few months to make sure you are indeed headed in the right direction. Sometimes our GPS needs to do some "recalculating."

---

13 Morrison, Lieutenant General David. 2013. Speech at the United Nations International Women's Day Conference.

Have you started thinking about some of the people who may be a good fit for your personal board? See which of the following fourteen traits (divided into four categories) each of your "board prospects" possesses.

	Advisor Name	Board Seat	Date	
	>	>	>	Pass Y/N?
1	Personal Traits	Compatibility and Personal Connection	Dealbreakers	
2		Alignment of Values, Balance, and Empathy	Dealbreakers	
3		Trustworthiness and Psychological Safety	Dealbreakers	
4	Interaction Style	Communication and Feedback Style	Critical - Flexible	
5		Commitment and Empowerment	Critical - Flexible	
6		Accountability and Flexibility	Critical - Flexible	
7		Objectivity and Constructive Criticism	Critical - Flexible	
8	Professional Alignment	Expertise	Desired Traits	
9		Track Record and Experience	Desired Traits	
10		Long-Term Vision and Continuing Education	Desired Traits	
11	External Factors	Availability	Major Consideration	
12		Cultural Sensitivity	Major Consideration	
13		Diversity	Major Consideration	
14		Influence and Network	Major Consideration	

Figure 7: Table outlining the traits you may look for and ask about with board member prospects while determining if the two of you could or should build a lasting relationship.

You can find a template for this table on the companion website. Complete a soft copy for each of your board member prospects or print it out!

The nonnegotiable details are the personal traits. These dealbreaker items concentrate on assessing whether you have compatibility and can genuinely form a personal connection. It's also crucial to align values, comprehend what balance means to them, and understand their levels of empathy. Completing the list of nonnegotiable traits are trustworthiness and psychological safety.

Next, we should assess their interaction style which includes critical (but perhaps flexible) traits. Make sure to understand and get a feel for their communication and feedback style. Gauge their commitment to supporting you and how they will empower you to grow over time. Ask about their approaches to accountability and flexibility. Last, but not least, discuss "what 'good' looks like" when it comes to constructive criticism.

The third set of traits concerns professional alignment, and we can think of these as the "desired skills" on a résumé. These are the "nice to have" items. It's important to learn about their professional expertise, track record, and experience in guiding others. Ask questions to understand their long-term professional vision and their thoughts on continuing education.

The fourth and final set of traits comprises external factors including but not limited to their availability to meet, cultural sensitivity, views and actions around diversity, and influence and network (i.e., the connections and introductions they can make).

Now we can dive a bit deeper into each of these categories of traits and get a feel for some of the things to think about and consider when evaluating each board prospect on our journey.

Personal Traits (The Dealbreakers)

Do you have a good fit with this individual, and is there compatibility and a personal connection? Byron is a friend and sponsor of mine, and he has a way of connecting with people I have never seen before—he finds a shared chemistry with each person he meets. For my last birthday, he gifted me a copy of the book *Bluefishing: The Art of Making Things Happen,* which references the concept of a "chug test," which is a concept that makes you think about whether or not you would actually sit down and have a drink (of your choice) with this person, or would that experience be excruciating to bear.

The next nonnegotiable is ensuring that you have aligned values and are in sync with their approach to work–life integration and overall balance. Do they match your style and how you operate? Evaluate whether their personal and professional values align with yours. What about their work ethic? Consider their level of empathy and emotional intelligence, especially their capacity to provide support during challenges. I recall a situation where I genuinely liked the person I was considering for my board, but their transactional, me-first approach to interactions was off-putting. They were affluent and widely regarded as successful, but they just weren't the right fit for me.

Some of the potential mentors that I found just didn't feel right, and I never could be at ease with them. This is tough for me to share as an engineer because I like to quantify everything, but sometimes there just is not a fit. If you're still on the fence about someone, it might come down to the third dealbreaker: trustworthiness and (lack of) psychological safety. Evaluate their trustworthiness and the level of confidentiality you can maintain. Can you be open with them, and do you trust them to keep things you share to themselves?

Interaction Style (Critical but Perhaps Flexible)

Get a feel for their communication and feedback styles early on. Understand their preferred methods of communication and their inclinations for giving and receiving feedback. Can you both listen effectively? Do they communicate in a way that you can comprehend and apply? I experienced a breakthrough when I found board members who could adjust their level of detail; I typically preferred those who were concise and to the point. Inquiring about their conversational style helped me discern what truly worked best. When certain prospects tended to ramble, I realized they weren't a great fit for me.

Another aspect not to be taken lightly is their commitment to your growth and their approach to empowering you. Evaluate their dedication to your development and success, as well as their ability to inspire and enable you to reach your full potential. Are they genuinely "in" to assist you? As we discussed earlier, this distinguishes a friend or family member from an advisor—meeting this criterion means they are prepared to have difficult conversations with you, even if their words might initially cause discomfort.

The best board members will always prioritize accountability and, when necessary, bring flexibility to the relationship. Determine their willingness to challenge you and hold you accountable for your goals and actions. Consider their flexibility in adapting to your evolving needs and goals. You will hear me say this many more times in the book: it's not one-size-fits-all, and the processes that grow stagnant are unlikely to flourish!

You may have more items on your own "super-important-but-somewhat-flexible" list, but the final one for this section is the person's objectivity and ability to provide constructive criticism. Evaluate their ability to provide objective and unbiased guidance and constructive criticism to help you grow.

Professional Alignment (Desired Traits, Nice to Have)

As with anyone from whom you seek professional advice, it's important to determine if they genuinely have expertise in the areas where you require guidance. Evaluate their field of expertise and how it aligns with your goals and needs.

Have they won in their careers, and have they succeeded in a way that you find valuable from a growth and learning perspective? Ask about their track record and work experiences as well as experiences when guiding and mentoring others. Evaluate their track record of supporting others in achieving their goals. Consider their own professional experience and track record of professional success.

Finally, evaluate their ability to provide guidance for long-term career planning and vision. Consider their dedication to their own continuous learning and professional development.

External Factors (Major Considerations)

This final section is by no means of less importance than the items mentioned above, and it is up to you how you weigh these items—all of which could indeed be dealbreakers if you value them highly enough.

Do they have time? Consider their availability for meetings, discussions, and support. Then, consider their cultural background and their ability to provide diverse perspectives. Relatedly, ensure diversity in the composition of your board to foster inclusive and well-rounded insights. Lastly, assess their influence and connections within your industry or desired field, determine whether these could benefit your career or other endeavors, and consider if they can introduce you to other supportive individuals in their network.

Action and Reflection

In closing Chapter 3, there are a few items to reflect on:

1. Who are some of your first mentors who could get added to your PBA?

2. Have you been a mentor to somebody else?

3. Take time to reflect on your personal and professional goals. Create a list of individuals who possess the skills, knowledge, and/or experiences that align with your aspirations. If you want bonus points, you can reach out to them and explore the possibility of forming mentorship relationships. However, if you're not sure how to get that conversation started, don't worry, we will cover this process soon.

Space for your notes and reflection.

CHAPTER 4

UNDERSTANDING THE PUZZLE PIECES OF YOUR BOARD

"What people say, what people do, and what people say they do are entirely different things."

Margaret Mead, a renowned cultural anthropologist whose observations became the compass for understanding society and human behavior in the twentieth century

Charting the course for your PBA is akin to assembling the intricate maps used by sailors of old. Each board member is a unique landmark, guiding you through the vast ocean of your personal and professional journey. As we sail through our careers, we encounter a diverse fleet of mentors, each anchoring us in different waters and guiding us through various tides and winds. This chapter is your sextant, offering precise insights into the myriad roles and responsibilities these individuals can undertake. With this knowledge, you'll be better equipped to gather a crew that steers your ship steadily toward your desired horizon.

Not One-Size-Fits-All

Now that you've made it a few chapters into this book, you may be thinking, "Wow, this is a lot." Or maybe you are thinking that you have this all under control and are well on your way to success. Perhaps you are like most readers and have become curiously optimistic about how to proceed. Think about the words of Bruce Lee . . .

"Absorb what is useful,
discard what is not, and
add what is uniquely your own."

This quote is to remind each of us as we read that this book is a guide and a path for us to follow. You may come up with other ideas and concepts along the way that make things more applicable to your life or situation. Please use these concepts as building blocks and a foundation; the book alone cannot guarantee your success. Only what you take from it and apply can accomplish that!

Figure 8: Photo of the Bruce Lee statue,
taken by Pete while studying in Hong Kong in 2013.

You may wind up having a few personal boards of advisors and perhaps a more in-depth career map than some or most of your peers—that is ok! If you are in a career transition, this experience will be slightly different for you. If you are looking to grow and climb the ladder within your current organization, you may take a different approach to thinking about how to populate your board. If you are winding down in your career, you may be on many boards of others, but you may not be as energized about building or revising your own board. We love to pay it forward!

It's OK to take a few moments to create a mental inventory of where you are today, what you truly need most, and how that impacts and influences the next several years of your journey. Heck, I've made at least a dozen career maps since college and have facilitated the personal board workshop more than fifty times before publishing this book.

Board Member Support Throughout Your Career

The figure below illustrates the timeline of your board's growth and development (from left to right). The size of the circles indicates how much time you will spend with each board seat at various career stages, with larger circles meaning more time spent with that particular board member. The board layout in this book accommodates eight seats (with ten options to choose from), allowing you to adjust this approach according to what serves you best at each specific point in your career journey. Your personal board will be dynamic, evolving in tandem with your career. It's OK to add and remove board members over time—each person enters your life at the right moment for the right reason!

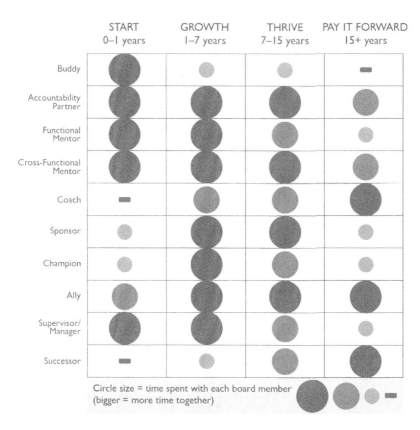

Figure 9: Visual representation of how dynamic the roles of board members can be throughout the course of someone's career.

Board Seat Details (Matrix)

As we plot each role on your personal board, the table in Figure 10 will be updated, serving as both a chart for the roles and a compass pointing you in the direction of your career goals. Remember, in the sea of opportunities, every element is interconnected, guiding you to your professional destination.

	Ch.	Experience	Internal vs External	Your Goal with Them	Career Map Focus	Their Background (found where)	Meeting Frequency (over time)
Buddy	10						
Accountability Partner	11						
Functional Mentor	12						
Cross-Functional Mentor	13		We will complete this table in Part II of the book and populate with detailed suggestions for each of the roles on your **PBA**.				
Coach	14						
Sponsor	15						
Champion	16						
Ally	17						
Supervisor/ Manager	18						
Successor	19						

Figure 10: Example of the table that we will build out for each board seat in Part II.

You may want to print out a copy of this table before getting into Part II to take notes as we dive into each board seat.

"With great power comes great responsibility."

Uncle Ben, a character in the Spider-Man movie

Visualizing Your Board

The image below will be referenced several more times throughout this book, helping you understand how to build out each of the seats on your very own PBA. They say a picture is worth a thousand words, so let's make things a bit easier and have some fun with it!

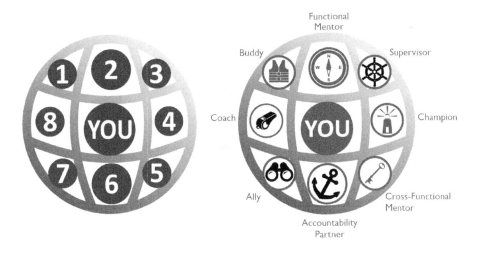

Figure 11: Graphic adding some structure to your personal board and (on the right) an example of what your board may look like in the middle of your career.

Action and Reflection

As we conclude Chapter 4, and you've begun to envision what your personal board might resemble, including some of the initial seats to fill, it's beneficial to understand what you're seeking from each of these individuals—beyond engaging conversations and discussions, of course. We'll delve into that shortly! The upcoming chapter explores career maps, offering a strategy to trace where we've been, where we are, and where we aim to head in the future. Armed with the beginnings of a plan or map, our guides can then provide substantial feedback, assisting us in navigating toward our desired destinations!

1. Which eight (of the ten) seats do you think are most needed at this stage of your professional development journey?

2. Would it make sense to have multiple boards for various aspects of your life or journey?

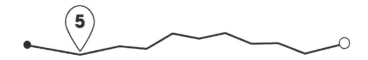

CHAPTER 5

WHAT IS A CAREER MAP?

*"Maps are great when you know where
you want to go, but creating a map on your own
can be next to impossible when you have little
to no idea what lies ahead!"*

Pete Schramm

We just learned about some of the people who can help us grow on our professional journey, so now we will dive into some of the things to discuss with them! The nautical adventure continues with a focus on career cartography in this chapter. We are going to build out a map of our own professional plans together, and the PBA is the resource that we will lean on to iterate on this valuable navigational resource over time. Our career maps help us outline what we have done, what we are doing, and what we aspire to do in the future. We can think of this as an exercise for visualizing our résumé and forecasting how we'd like to reshape it.

In a very basic sense, your career map may initially look something like the figure below.

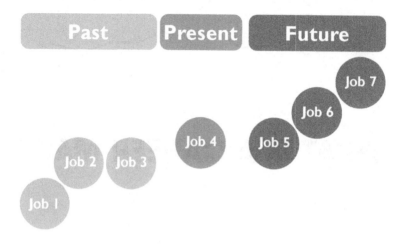

Figure 12: The most basic visualization of a career map showing the jobs you have had, the job you have, and the jobs you think you may have in the future.

But let's face it: change is the only thing that is for certain. The figure below shows what a more realistic career map might look like. The future often has a lot of variability!

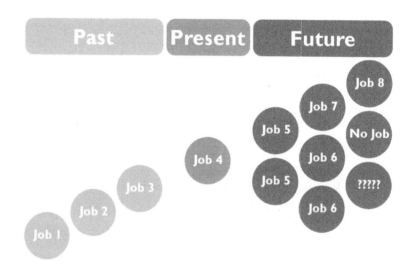

Figure 13: A more realistic visualization of a career map showing the options for various jobs that you may have in the future.

Individual Development Plans (IDPs), utilized by many leaders in the talent development space, serve as collaborative tools between an employee and their manager to plan career growth. While the employee primarily owns the outcome, both parties play a role in crafting and implementing the plan. The primary objectives of an IDP include maintaining job proficiency, charting a career path by identifying new skills, and supporting the organization's broader mission. These plans offer mutual benefits: employees receive a clear path for personal and career development, while organizations ensure their workforce is evolving in line with their goals. It's important to note that IDPs are flexible, evolving based on performance reviews and changing job roles. Essentially, while not a novel concept, IDPs remain a cornerstone for methodical and structured career advancement.

Knowing Thyself First

Before we dive into the lifecycle stages of your board-building process, we must start with you! What are you all about, and why? The quote below from the ancient Chinese philosopher and founder of Taoism, Lao Tzu, is special, one that we can all reflect on throughout our entire professional journeys:

> *"Knowing others is intelligence;*
> *knowing yourself is true wisdom.*
> *Mastering others is strength;*
> *Mastering yourself is true power."*

What's Your Why?

No one else can tell you what your "why" or your purpose is; this is intrinsic. Others can help you uncover your why, and they can guide you on your journey, but you have to take the first steps.

What is something that makes you jump out of bed in the morning, you get so excited about this concept or activity?

What makes you stay up late past your bedtime working on something? This is the sort of activity that puts you into a flow state, where sleep is forgotten. (I'm not suggesting this is a healthy approach, but it does seem to happen at times!)

What would you do if money were not an issue? Loans are paid, food is covered, rent is $0, and you do not "need" money. How would you spend your time?

Based on hundreds of conversations, I have found that most millennials and Gen Zers say they want to travel, while most Gen Xers and boomers say they would pursue a different job or spend more time with family. Did any of those come to mind for you? Is that what you genuinely want to do, or are you simply defaulting to someone else's goal?

Goals for You

You have probably heard about making SMART[14] goals for various projects and initiatives, and certain leaders or mentors may have challenged you to refine them time and time again making them SMART(Y). SMART(Y) goals are clearly defined, easy to understand, and can be "marked as done" without confusion.

I like to add "Y" to this acronym, signifying that the goal is Yours—it is personal. It's crucial that this goal isn't just a copy-and-paste from another goal you heard about or one placed on your to-do list by someone else. Sure, it's fine to adopt principles and best practices from others, but consider whether the goal should or could be altered, updated, or refined to truly become your goal!

Later parts of the book delve into SMARTY goals for your career over time and discuss how to break down goals with each person on your board. We've covered specifics, measurements, and achievability. This is a reminder for you to determine whether building your PBA is a current priority, if it's relevant for this stage of your journey, and if the time is right. Are you ready for this to be about your growth and development, not just something your boss or another leader instructed you to do— copy-and-paste fashion to check a box and move on? This concept can truly change your life when executed correctly.

I didn't realize the value of this concept until I inadvertently started consulting what would become my PBA. I relied on my Buddy when planning the next steps in my career journey—we already had a strong pre-existing relationship,

14 S.M.A.R.T. GOALS Trademark of LEADERSHIP MANAGEMENT INTERNATIONAL, INC. - Registration Number 3452666 - Serial Number 77273042 :: Justia Trademarks. SMART Goals is a trademarked phrase. Check out their work for more information on SMART goals!

so it was easy. I confided in my Champion when something didn't feel right on a specific project, and when my alignment with my leader faltered, prompting the Buddy chat about the next steps in my career map.

Figure 14: Acronym for SMARTY goals.

Specific - What are you getting done, who is part of this, why are you doing this, and where will this get done (when is in the "T" part of this process)?

Measurable - Think about the metrics required to track this goal. Can you gather a baseline today and show progress over time? What measurement needs to be "filled" for successful completion?

Achievable - Is this something that you can complete and accomplish with the resources that you have?

Realistic/Relevant - Does this *actually* need to be tracked in the grand scheme of things? Consider the positive impact and outcome upon completion: Will it have a small, medium, or large benefit?

Timely - By when will this goal be completed? Is it reasonable to set an Estimated Completion Date (ECD) within the next week, month, or quarter? Ideally you will have multiple "sub-goals" to complete within a year.

Yours - This is all about you, and if you have just copied and pasted a goal from someone else or another source, it may not actually be for *you*.

Discovering Ikigai: Unearthing Your True Purpose

In the journey to map our career trajectory, understanding our innermost desires, passions, and purpose is paramount. One concept that provides a profound lens to this self-exploration is *ikigai*, a Japanese term that translates to "reason for being."

At the heart of ikigai lies the intersection of four primary elements:

1. **What you love (your passion)**
2. **What the world needs (your mission)**
3. **What you are good at (your vocation)**
4. **What you can be paid for (your profession)**

I like to reference the Venn diagram from Michael Hartzell where these elements overlap, and right in the center, you'll find ikigai—a harmonious point where personal satisfaction meets the needs of the world around us. Finding these answers is not easy, and some people search for a full lifetime without really achieving this. Others don't even know what they should be looking for!

Figure 15: My take on the ikigai diagram, building from Michael Hartzell's work.

This planning step is perhaps the most important aspect of your career map to effectively populate your own map and navigate your optimal professional development journey. The companion website has a template that can be populated.

Ikigai and Your Career Map

Building a career map that encompasses the past, present, and future requires more than just plotting professional milestones. It demands an understanding of what truly drives us, what we yearn for, and what brings us genuine fulfillment.

Past: Reflecting on our past experiences through the ikigai framework allows us to identify patterns. What roles or tasks have ignited passion? In what areas did we find ourselves most skilled? Recognizing these can shed light on our true vocations and missed opportunities.

Present: In our current roles, ikigai can serve as a compass. Are we aligning with what we love and what we're good at? If there's a mismatch, understanding our ikigai can help reorient our trajectory, ensuring we're not just working for a paycheck but for a deeper, more fulfilling purpose.

Future: When plotting the future of our career, ikigai encourages us to envision a path where we not only excel professionally but also contribute positively to the world. This ensures our profession aligns closely with our mission.

Ikigai and Your Personal Boards of Advisors

As you journey to uncover your ikigai, your PBA plays a crucial role. These mentors and guides can provide insights into recognizing your passions, honing your skills, and aligning with a mission that resonates. Through their varied experiences and perspectives, they can shed light on blind spots, offer guidance when there's a misalignment, and celebrate with you as you discover and live your ikigai.

I learned a lot more about the depth and difficulty of this process when I left the United States for the first time in my life. I spent six months in Hong Kong with people from more than thirty countries, and, as you may have guessed, I did my best to learn about their backgrounds, dreams, and aspirations. I saw firsthand how many others were influenced by those who came before them, such as parents, siblings, classmates, teammates, and peers in previous jobs. Most knew that they did not want to continue on the path they were headed down, but they felt it had already been decided for them. Here are a few examples:

- **Profession Without Passion or Mission:** Within the automobile industry, Martin was on a trajectory toward executive status, emulating his father. Yet beneath the surface, there was turmoil. Expectations weighed heavily on him, and he felt lost without a roadmap or a confidant to guide him.

- **Vocation Without Clarity:** Lance felt a pressing need to attend business school and ascend to leadership. But this path, influenced by external voices, was shrouded in ambiguity. What did leadership truly mean to him?

- **Passion Without Vocation:** Oscar yearned for a life filled with joy and simplicity. Yet, the prestigious financial allure of New York's banking sector beckoned him. Caught between personal desires and professional allure, he was at a crossroads.

- **The Quest for Purpose:** Arturo's journey was marked by profound introspection. He was on a relentless quest, not just for a career, but for a purpose that resonated with the core of who he was.

Your "why" and your purpose are crucial to your personal and professional development journey. You will continue to learn that the stronger your "why" and purpose are, the more resilient you become. When you ignite your internal spark, there are few challenges you cannot take on. When you successfully couple your "why" with the right people on your personal board and develop your plan together, the opportunities that start developing can be limitless.

For those in search of more content on this topic, here are a few of my favorite sources. (A more detailed list is included in the Appendix.) Books like Viktor Frankl's Man's Search for Meaning *and Paulo Coelho's* The Alchemist *delve deep into the human psyche and the quest for purpose. Daniel Pink's* Drive *explores the intricacies of motivation, while Simon Sinek's works encourage us to "start with why." On the auditory front, podcasts such as NPR's* Hidden Brain *and* On Purpose with Jay Shetty *offer a blend of stories and expert advice, guiding listeners toward their own personal truths.*

Self-Discovery Tools

Throughout life, many of us embark on a journey to understand ourselves better, often using tools and assessments to gain insights into our innate strengths, preferences, and motivations. I began my exploration as early as eighth grade when an assessment suggested a culinary path due to my love of food. Later, during college, another nudge hinted at architecture, reflecting my passion for design and creativity. While I didn't follow these specific paths professionally, I've channeled these passions into innovative culinary creations at home and dedicated landscape projects on my farm.

Among the myriad tools available for such self-discovery, a few have been particularly enlightening for me. The StrengthsFinder (now CliftonStrengths®) highlights an individual's top strengths from thirty-four talent themes. The Emergenetics® Test offers a deep dive into thinking and behavioral preferences spanning seven distinct attributes. For those curious about work-related behaviors and motivations, the Predictive Index® provides valuable insights. The DiSC Profile®, although met with some academic skepticism, measures traits like dominance and conscientiousness. These are but a few of the many tools available, and a comprehensive list can be found in the Appendix of this book. It's worth noting that while some of these assessments cost money, the investment often proves invaluable, especially when reviewed alongside a trained coach. If you're ever in need of guidance post-assessment, don't hesitate to seek out a coach.

The Quadrants of Your Career Map

Now it's time to add some more structure to this map concept! The image below shows what a more detailed career map template may look like. As this image builds up, you will see that there are still some unknowns, and that is to be expected. The major takeaway is to have a plan in place and have something to iterate on over time with your board members. As we just saw, there are multiple options for some of the "future" sections here, and the purpose is to offer flexibility—our priorities can and likely will shift as we progress. After we walk through some examples of completing this table, I will lay out the step-by-step process that you can take when populating this map yourself.

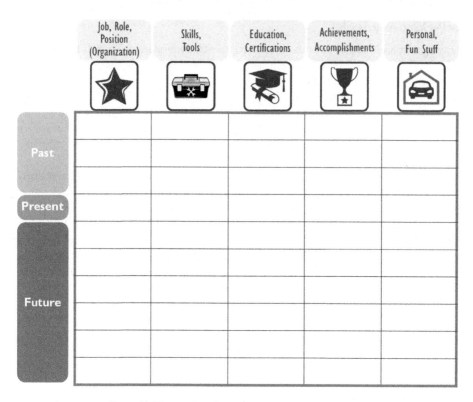

Figure 16: The template for a career map that we will follow
and populate throughout this chapter.

**The companion website has a template that can be followed as we
progress through this chapter.**

Job, Role, and Position (Organization)

In the first column of the career map, we are going to document the roles you have held over the years and the roles you plan to hold in the future. It is important to remind ourselves of what we have done in the past, so we have the opportunity to reflect and also see how many career journeys truly do build on themselves, sometimes even without intentional planning.

Another important aspect to be aware of in this process is that *future* steps should have multiple options for each of the opportunities ahead of us. Later I will share a sample of the career map I developed in 2017 to help bring all this together.

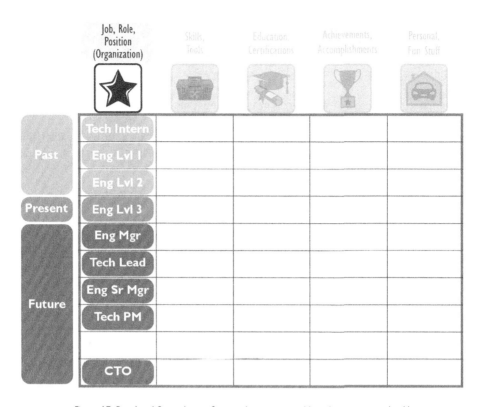

Job, Role, Position (Organization)	Skills, Tools	Education, Certifications	Achievements, Accomplishments	Personal, Fun Stuff
Tech Intern				
Eng Lvl 1				
Eng Lvl 2				
Eng Lvl 3				
Eng Mgr				
Tech Lead				
Eng Sr Mgr				
Tech PM				
CTO				

Figure 17: Populated first column of a sample career map. Note that your map should have multiple options for each of the future blocks.

When building out the first column of your map, you may realize that some of the future roles and positions could move you laterally in a role (with no promotion or increase in salary), move you into a higher pay range, or increase your responsibility without a higher salary (not ideal, but it does happen). Ideally, you are able to take the role that is best for you. It is important to remember here that lateral moves are OK and that many people took a new role in a new industry in a new company with a lower salary at many points in their career. Figure 18 helps us visualize this concept of what the future jobs may hold when thinking about leveling up, increasing salary, changing companies, and switching industries.

For example, if you are currently a program manager, you may move vertically into roles such as senior program manager, then program director, followed by a vice president of programs/operations role, and then chief executive officer (CEO). If you opt to move laterally at any point, you may transition into roles such as business development manager, capture manager, product manager, operations manager, or even a technical program manager.

The transition from "Job 4" to the various "Job 5" options portrays the various paths we may take; to the left means that we kept the same salary and decreased in level, perhaps due to an organization downsizing. The "Job 5" circle to the right tells that the position increased in level and responsibility without a salary increase. This may happen if a promotion takes place outside of a scheduled review and pay increase cycle. The "Job 5" circle directly above the current "Job 4" role shows that this employee stayed at the same level and position and also got a pay raise.

It is important to note that we will go through various phases of professional development and at times, an increase in responsibility is no longer attractive or conducive to the life we want to live. In this case, you may strive to only move up instead of up and to the right. If you do not move right, you may take longer to reach the next job further to the right.

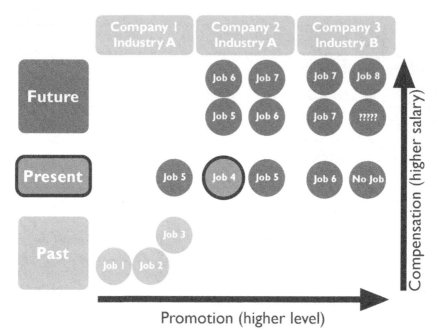

Figure 18: Breakout of the first column of the career map that we are populating. There are various ways that you can progress through your career. Note that the image flips the past/present/future details compared to the previous image to represent more clearly an "onwards and upwards" professional growth trajectory.

The companion website has a template that can be populated as you plan out potential career paths. This is a great exercise to do with your Champion, Supervisor, or Functional Mentor (more on this in Part II).

Skills and Tools

The second column explores the skills and technical requirements associated with each quadrant of your career map (job/role, skills, education/certifications/accomplishments, and personal milestones/hobbies). This is what you learned and took with you along your path; these skills and abilities are now part of you! Examples include (but are in no way limited to) project management, leadership development, virtual communication, cost account management, managing a $500,000 annual budget, and managing a team of six people.

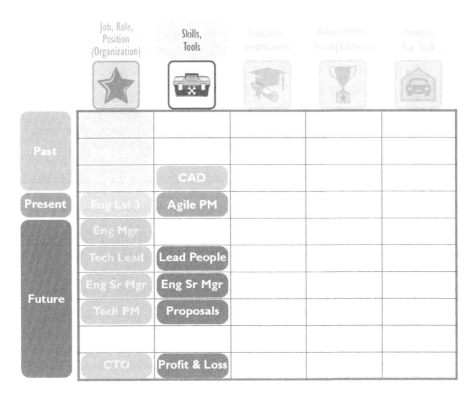

Figure 19: This is a breakout of the second column of the career map. Your map should have multiple options for the future blocks at this stage and for the following columns as well.

Education and Certifications

As we move across the map from left to right, we highlight the significance of certifications, training, and milestones as markers of your progress and professional growth. This is where we see external, structured, professional development and other formal types of training happening. This column also feeds into the national push for upskilling, reskilling, and what I like to call "new skilling." Examples include (but again are not limited to) an MBA completed at Penn State University, PMP certification, and Lean Six Sigma Black Belt certification.

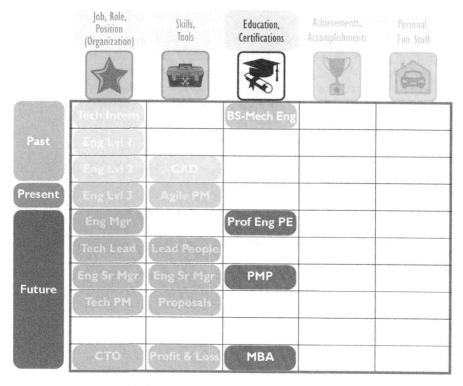

	Job, Role, Position (Organization)	Skills, Tools	Education, Certifications	Achievements, Accomplishments	Personal, Fun Stuff
Past	Tech Intern		BS-Mech Eng		
	Eng Lvl 1				
	Eng Lvl 2	CAD			
Present	Eng Lvl 3	Agile PM			
Future	Eng Mgr		Prof Eng PE		
	Tech Lead	Lead People			
	Eng Sr Mgr	Eng Sr Mgr	PMP		
	Tech PM	Proposals			
	CTO	Profit & Loss	MBA		

Figure 20: This is a breakout of the third column of the career map.

Achievements and Accomplishments

The last of the core quadrants tracks achievements and accomplishments. These are outcomes and results, often ones that must be left behind when you move on from a position or company, and they are often things others will brag about on your behalf. This is another section where our PBA can significantly assist in looking ahead toward the "things we need to do" to reach new heights and continue growing professionally.

This is where our PBA can be particularly helpful, guiding us toward the kinds of achievements we should pursue to attain future jobs and positions. You might populate your map with brief descriptions of a cost-saving initiative you completed, a large proposal that you managed, a new process that you developed and implemented, or the number of people that you interviewed or hired. As you look to the future blocks of the map, you may aim to increase the number or impact of previous achievements, or you might want to add more challenging accomplishments to your map!

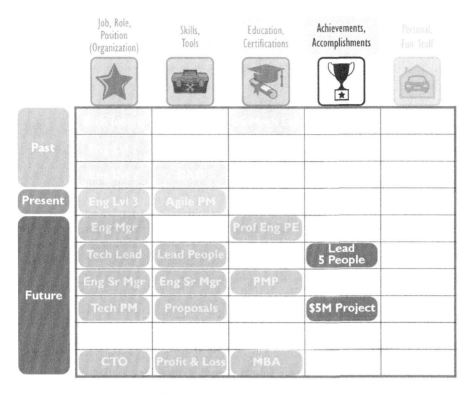

Job, Role, Position (Organization)	Skills, Tools	Education, Certifications	Achievements, Accomplishments	Personal, Fun Stuff
Eng Lvl 3	Agile PM			
Eng Mgr		Prof Eng PE		
Tech Lead	Lead People		Lead 5 People	
Eng Sr Mgr	Eng Sr Mgr	PMP		
Tech PM	Proposals		$5M Project	
CTO	Profit & Loss	MBA		

Figure 21: Breakout of the fourth and final "professional" column of the career map.

Hobbies and Personal Interests

I know that "quadrants" mean four items, so think of the prior four sections as the career quadrants and this fifth section as the column that pulls the whole map together. This is the place where we track fun activities outside of work and any major nonwork goals and objectives for the future. Think about some of the things you want to accomplish in your life outside of work. Outside the remaining content in this chapter, this quadrant will not be addressed elsewhere in this book. I'm not here to tell you how to live your life, but I do want to remind you that it is imperative to plan out the life you want and to set goals and meet them. Make sure that you build in time for you.

Justifying "Personal Stuff" on a Professional Development Journey

In our quest for professional success, it's easy to fall into the trap of overworking. Modern work culture, particularly in high-pressure industries, often glorifies long hours. I've been a culprit of this for years and have battled burnout many times. However, research indicates there's a tipping point after which more hours don't translate to more productivity. In fact, they can have the opposite effect.

A study by John Pencavel of Stanford University highlighted that productivity per hour declines sharply when a person works more than fifty hours a week.[15] After fifty-five hours, the productivity drop is so significant that there's no point in working any more. That is, someone who works seventy hours produces nothing more with those extra fifteen hours. I know that some weeks require longer hours, but see if you can scale back to what science is trying to tell us!

Data from the Organisation for Economic Co-operation and Development (OECD) also indicate that shorter work hours can correlate with higher productivity.[16] For instance, countries like Germany and Norway, which have shorter workweeks, often report higher productivity levels than nations with longer working hours.

It's not just about productivity either. Long work hours have been linked to a range of health problems, from increased risk of heart disease (one of the top reasons for death in corporate leaders) to heightened stress levels.[17] Moreover, working excessively can lead to burnout, a state of physical or emotional exhaustion, particularly if accompanied by a sense of reduced accomplishment and loss of personal identity.[18]

As a result, incorporating personal interests, hobbies, and fun activities outside of work into our career maps isn't just about relaxation. These activities can serve as a buffer against the negative effects of job stress and can enhance well-being, creativity, and even job performance.[19] As you chart your career map, ensure you carve out time for the things that rejuvenate you, whether that's reading, knitting, playing basketball, volunteering, hiking, traveling, learning to play guitar, dating, or spending time with loved ones. After all, a well-rounded individual is often a more productive and happier one.

15 Pencavel, J. (2014). The Productivity of Working Hours. The Economic Journal, 125(589), 2052-2076.

16 Organisation for Economic Co-operation and Development. (2019). Hours worked. OECD Data.

17 Virtanen, M., Heikkilä, K., Jokela, M., Ferrie, J. E., Batty, G. D., Vahtera, J., & Kivimäki, M. (2012). Long working hours and coronary heart disease: a systematic review and meta-analysis. American journal of epidemiology, 176(7), 586-596.

18 Maslach, C., Schaufeli, W. B., & Leiter, M. P. (2001). Job burnout. Annual review of psychology, 52(1), 397-422.

19 Sturges, J. (2012). Crafting a balance between work and leisure. Journal of Occupational and Organizational Psychology, 85(2), 207-230.

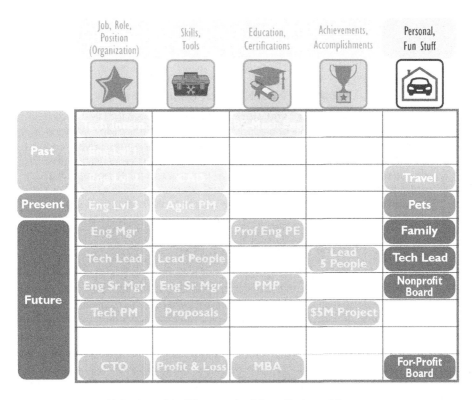

Figure 22: Breakout of the fifth, personal and fun stuff column of the career map.
Please add in multiple options on this one!

The companion website lists a few examples of completed career maps that might be helpful to look at when building out the first drafts of your own map.

Additional Inputs and Quadrants

You may have a few other items to include for the ideal career map for you—location, salary, and industry are a few possibilities. For now, you may add these to your fourth column, "Achievements and Accomplishments." However, the cool part about using the career companion website is that as the need for an additional quadrant grows and becomes more prevalent to a larger user base, we can add it! So, if you find yourself wanting to add a lot of items in a particular category that is not yet reflected, please reach out and let me know by completing the "Share Your Story" form on the companion website.

People as Future Career Map Pieces

Wild concept alert! What if you were to add a few people that you aspire to be like on some of the future portions of your career map? Perhaps there is a manager you admire in a certain position you covet, and you'd like to be in their shoes in the next four to eight years. A creative way to populate your board could be with names of other people. Just make sure your PBA knows who these individuals are, so they can help provide more insight and guidance on how to make that plan a reality.

The Organic Nature of Our Career Map

A fulfilling career is often one that aligns with your passions and leverages your unique strengths. Identifying these elements and incorporating them into your career map can lead to a more satisfying and successful professional journey. Your personal board members can assist in this process, helping you identify and leverage your unique talents, interests, and aspirations. Reflect on the earlier questions: If money or financial commitments were not a concern, how would you spend your time? What activities ignite your passion? Can you incorporate these elements into your future roles, skills, or certifications? Remember, it's OK to iterate and refine your map as you gain more clarity about your passions and strengths.

Your career is more than just a series of jobs—it's a reflection of your purpose and mission. Keeping these elements at the forefront of your career map ensures that your professional journey aligns with your core values and contributes to your overall life goals. Your personal board can help you maintain this alignment, guiding you to make career choices that resonate with your mission and values. They can also provide perspective when you face decisions that challenge your commitment to your purpose, helping you navigate these situations with integrity.

I remember interviewing for a job where I was competing against two other candidates, each with almost fourteen more years of experience than I had. I consulted my board in advance and reviewed my career map with them. I developed my talking points for the myriad chapters of my professional path, going all the way back to my full-time internship work. After the interviews, it was decided that none of us would get the job, as it would have directly competed with Elon Musk's projects!

In a recent workshop, a few CEOs decided to incorporate this career map concept into their interview process, asking certain prospects to complete a career map during their interview. This approach gave the leaders a chance to see what each candidate was truly seeking to accomplish. It also demonstrated that the organization was willing to help the candidate develop professionally, build out their career map, and turn some of their ideas and concepts into reality!

In the ever-evolving landscape of professional life, adaptability is key. Your career map is not a rigid blueprint but a flexible guide that evolves with your experiences, your aspirations, and the changing dynamics of the professional world. It's essential to embrace change and remain open to new possibilities. Your PBA plays a crucial role here, providing support and guidance during transitions, helping you adapt your career map to changing circumstances, and ensuring that you remain resilient in the face of unexpected challenges.

Notice how the icons (previously detailed in Figure 5 of Chapter 1) of some of the board seats are shown in Figure 23. Each person can help in a specific manner along the way. Part II of the book covers how each board member adds unique value to the career map at various points in your career.

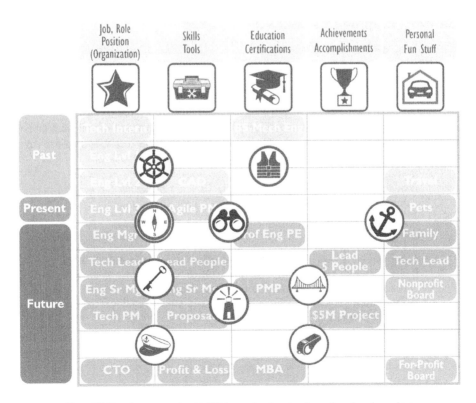

Figure 23: Sample career map with PBA icons at various locations where board members can provide specific guidance and support.

The companion website shares a few examples of where specific board members can help guide our mapping process. You may also want to use the career map worksheet to identify where you have gaps in your map today. It may also be a good time to explore adding a person's name to a future block on your career map—somebody who is in a position or has achieved certain things that you wish to do.

As you develop your career map, remember that it should be a unique reflection of your journey. While you can draw inspiration from others, avoid replicating someone else's map entirely. Your career map should be tailored to your individual aspirations, strengths, and circumstances. Also, consider your "nonnegotiables"—those core values, commitments, or requirements that you are not willing to compromise. These elements can serve as your guiding principles, ensuring that your career path aligns with what matters most to you.

Career Mapping Process, Step by Step

After delivering a few dozen workshops with the career map, I realized that a bit of guidance and step-by-step instruction was very helpful to "first-time career cartographers." You can take a bottom-up approach, a top-down approach, or a hybrid approach. Bottom-up means that you start at the bottom of your map (the end of your career) and work your way back to the present. Top-down means that you build forward from the present iteratively, adding what you plan to do next until eventually getting to the end of your career. The most popular approach that I've seen for building an initial career map follows these steps.

1. In most instances, it's best to go back to your first experiences after high school graduation (approximately 18 years old). This can include summer jobs and internships.

2. Populate the "Past" column one for your "Job, Role, Position (Organization)."

3. Next, populate the "Past" portions of columns two, three, four, and five. (Note that others find it very helpful to first fill out column five, "Personal, Fun Stuff," when they dive into this exercise. If you get stuck, try that approach, and you may see how the pieces really do come together and all build up over time!)

4. Populate the "Present" row, adding details for all columns.

5. Now you can choose between a bottom-up or top-down approach: either fill out the very next step of the "Future" portion of your map or go to the end of your map and work backward.

6. As you build up the "Future" pieces of the map, you will add a few options in each of the cells. It is important to have backups in case things do not go exactly as planned.

7. Start sharing your map with others and begin iterating! Just like with a résumé or any other strategic plan, I find it helpful to save a copy each time so you can see the progress over time.

8. Make sure each row on the career map is in alignment with your overall goals, purpose, and ikigai.

A suggested cadence for reviewing your career map is every three to six months. Earlier in your career, you'll want to do this more frequently, as there will likely be more decision points and variables to plan out versus later in life.

There is a career mapping checklist available on the companion website to reference in this process and guide you through the steps as well.

Now it's time to show a full-fledged example. Figure 24 shows my career map from 2018. I was building this out while deciding whether to leave my current employer. The question mark on the far right shows that I was not planning out the personal aspects of my life and that I was just focused on work, work, work. It also shows that I was *not* consistently focusing on my key professional goal and referring to what my true aspirations were. Sure, I had fun and was able to go on adventures, but I am now working to be much more intentional about what matters most. I hope that as you are reading this section, you too are realizing that it is OK to take time for yourself and to have goals outside of work.

Pete Schramm Career Map (PAST)

Core Interests
- Continued learning & growth through stretch assignments
- Challenging, fast-paced environments with opportunities to learn & grow
- Utilization & development of team & business leadership skills
- Projects/initiatives involving Emerging & Disruptive Technology
- Projects/initiatives gathering corp focus and attention (good & bad)

Functional Required Competencies
- Earned Value Management
- Subcontract Management
- Multi-Disciplinary Team Leadership

Program Management Required Competencies
- Capture Management
- Earned Value Management
- Profit & Loss ($500M+)

	Positions		Skills & Competencies	Education, Training & Achievements
2010		**CUA**		
		Teamwork Skills	Fluid Dynamics	**Collegiate Athlete**
			Public Speaking	Basketball & Track
2011	**II-VI Inc** Stock Clerk Procurement	Data Analysis	Engineering Design	
		Experimental Design	Optical Engineering	**Study Abroad**
	AK Steel		Aerospace Design	
2012	Associate Maintenance Engineer	Research Proposal	FAR	**SAE Aero Design East** Competition - 19th Place (120 teams, 9 nations)
		Project Management	WIN Plan & Proposals Material Cost Planning	
2013	**Pierce** Assistant Project Manager	Leadership Development	Proposal Development	**BS** Mechanical Engineering
2014			Production Operations*** Union Interactions**	
	Lockheed Martin IS&GS		Training*** On-boarding*	**LM21** Green Belt Certified
2015	Material Cost Estimator		Management**	
	Lockheed Martin/EBS Environmental Sustainibility Engineer			**MS** Mechanical Engineering
	Lockheed Martin/MFC Supervisor Conformal Coating		PMT Dev Lead*** Cust Relations (Air Force)* Cust Relations (Navy)**	**LM21** Black Belt Trained
2016	**Lockheed Martin/MFC** PGS Supplier Quality Engineer		DCMA Interaction*** Quality Control***	**DOD** Secret Clearance
	Lockheed Martin/RMS VLS Quality Engineer (Lead QC POC Feb-July)		CAM	**LM21** Black Belt Certified
2017			Develop IMS* GRID Setup ROADS Risk Management**	**CAM** Trained & Certified
	Lockheed Martin/RMS MMSC Risk & Opportunity Program Manager		Hyperspectral Imaging Cust Relations (Army)	**PMP** (PMI) & **FPM** (LM)
2018				

Figure 24: The career map I developed in 2018 while working at Lockheed Martin. I planned to be COO by the year 2045!

Pete Schramm Career Map (FUTURE)

	Positions	Skills & Competencies	Education, Training & Achievements
2018	**Lockheed Martin/RMS** MMSC Risk & Opportunity Program Manager	?? Capture ?? Proposal ?? P&L Responsibility ?? Program Full Biz Lifecycle	DUO
2019 2020	**Lockheed Martin ???** 1. MMSC Dep PM 2. MMSC Prod Ops MPM 3. Flow Battery Asc PM 4. Laser/Cyber? 5. Work International? 6. TA?		Begin MBA ??? Master BB (Level 4) POLI PMDP
2021	**Lockheed Martin ???** 1. Program Manager 2. Ft Worth as Lv 5?	?? Shipbuilding ?? Planning ?? Mission Systems	

	Positions	Professional Interests	Personal Interests
2022	**Lockheed Martin (4-6)** 1. PM 2. BD	?? Consulting - is it possible to do any at LM?	?? Family - marriage ?? Children ?? Int'l Travel
2023 2024	**Lockheed Martin (5-7)** 1. PM 2. BD	?? Renewable Energy ?? Pittsburgh ?? Production - how can I get back to the prod floor where building HW?	?? Cont'd Work w/People ?? Respect in work place ?? Meaningful work ?? Challenge
2025 2026	**Lockheed Martin (6-8)** 1. PM 2. BD	?? Travel - any opportunity to travel internationally while I can?	
2027 2028		?? I would love to get more technical, lasers, CW, energy - engineering company	
2045	COO	?? Equity in company?	

Leveraging Your Personal Board's Guidance

Your personal board members are more than just advisors; they are thought partners who can help shape your career map. Their diverse insights, experiences, and perspectives can provide valuable input as you define your career path, helping you make informed decisions and envision future possibilities. Whether you're considering a career pivot, seeking to develop new skills, or exploring uncharted territories, your board members can offer critical thinking and strategic guidance.

In addition to being thought partners, your personal board members serve as *mentors* and *advisors*, guiding you through the process of mapping out your career. Their expertise, knowledge, and networks can support you in identifying potential roles, developing necessary skills, and achieving significant milestones. They can provide you with industry insights, career advice, and connections that can open doors to new opportunities, helping you navigate your career journey with confidence.

Your personal board members also serve as *accountability partners*, helping you stay focused and committed to your career map. Regular check-ins and progress discussions with your board members can ensure alignment with your career goals, keep you on track, and motivate you to push through challenges. Their role as accountability partners is crucial in maintaining your momentum and ensuring that your career map remains a living, actionable guide to your professional journey.

Steve was introduced to me while I was in college. He was a few years ahead of me, seemed like a good guy, and had been in the defense industry for a few years. We met for burgers, I asked him about his career, he shared a few tips and suggestions, and the rest is history. He became one of the first "pre-workplace" professional mentors that I had. Over time we became accountability partners for one another. His role shifted, and as we grew professionally, we realized that we could help one another in reviewing one another's career maps. We populated all five columns without realizing it. We still try our best to get a burger each year—now his family joins us too!

In the next chapter, we'll shift our focus to networking, diving deep into how authentic connections not only advance our careers but enrich our personal and professional narratives. The true essence of our journey lies not just in the path we envision, but in the people we meet along the way.

Action and Reflection

In closing Chapter 5, we are prepared to set sail with a much better idea of where we're heading. Some questions to consider:

1. When did you last update your own career map?

2. How long has it been since you reviewed your career map with somebody else?

3. Can you use a career map in preparation for an upcoming interview (either as the job seeker or the job filler)?

4. How close are you to finding your real ikigai today?

Space for your notes and reflection.

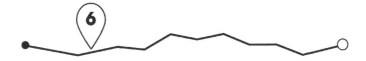

CHAPTER 6:

NAVIGATING NETWORKING WITH POTENTIAL MENTORS

"No one cares how much you know until they know how much you care."

President Theodore Roosevelt, the mustached maestro of the outdoors and 26th president of the United States

We need to find a personal board, and we need to build some kind of a career map with them. So now would be a great time to share some tips for finding people to network with and building relationships!

Some of the Wild Ways of Meeting People

While working at Lockheed Martin, I often embraced an unorthodox approach to networking. On certain days when I felt particularly adventurous, I decided to stride into random offices just to extend a friendly "hello." It felt audacious, but over time, it turned out to be one of my best strategies. Often, these spontaneous interactions led to invigorating conversations and forged unexpected bonds.

The water cooler, too, became a focal point of many unplanned encounters. I remember one particular day, as I took a break, I noticed a colleague standing alone. Drawing from my newfound confidence, I struck up a conversation with George. Later, it was Ken I conversed with. It wasn't long before we found common ground.

This principle of inclusivity extended beyond the office. During a Pittsburgh Human Resources Association bocce event, I noticed two people sitting alone and invited them to my table to mingle. Now I'm great friends with them and their families! A few weeks later, at a Pittsburgh Business Exchange event, I saw a man struggling to find an extension cord. I offered him a spare that I'd brought, and soon this mundane task had become a chance to connect; Rob and I became long-term friends and business partners. Similarly, a backyard barbecue invitation from my dear friend Ben evolved into more than five business deals with the people I met there, plus a few mentors who also helped in various capacities with this very book! In short, any interaction can be an opportunity for networking. Don't sleep on the random friendly gatherings or the advantage of "having a spare" at an event.

One key lesson I've learned is the power of referrals. Through a multiyear customer named Tasha, I was introduced to Angelo, who became a teammate, a friend, and then co-founder—all from sharing what I was searching for while Tasha and I were on a call working on a proposal. (In fact, our relationship was one of the ones that spun out from that backyard barbeque.)

One of the most influential relationships led me to one of the other most influential people in my life . . . two years after I started reaching out. Jim, Rosemary, and Tom suggested that I connect with Ethan and made an introduction that was met with radio silence for two years. (Yes, even when I followed up every few weeks, then months.) Another friend from a decade earlier, Brian, finally introduced me to Ethan at a Rotary meeting in Pittsburgh, and Ethan ultimately became more than a business partner, but it took time. Each introduction expanded my network in directions I hadn't anticipated.

One of the most serendipitous meetings occurred while I was walking out of a coffee shop with a potential future member of my PBA. After wrapping up a session with a prospective client, a very prominent business leader in the Pittsburgh area, a stranger named Frank approached me. His simple greeting, "Who are you, and what are you doing?" led to a phone call a few days later and eventually a lasting professional relationship, guidance, and business.

From these experiences, I understood that opportunity doesn't always knock on the door; sometimes it's waiting at the doors of coffee shops, in corridors, at barbecues, or a few years in the future. Whether they occur in my hometown or during my travels abroad, these everyday opportunities for networking are invaluable. They have reinforced my belief to always be open, always be present. You never know who's around the corner, waiting to change your life.

Where to Meet Board Prospects

"To define, move toward, and succeed in that future, you need to proactively build a far-flung network of people who live and work at the edge of your current world."

Linda A. Hill, Wallace Brett Donham Professor of Business Administration at Harvard Business School

Across our macro network, there are a few key places to look when exploring who may be good prospects for our board. A 2011 article in *Harvard Business Review* outlines three networks: (1) operational (people you interact with daily), (2) developmental (people you trust and turn to for advice), and (3) strategic (people who help you plan for the future). I like to think of identifying board prospects as a two-phase process: phase one is going through your existing networks to find people, and phase two is figuring out which relational network the board members will "reside" in.[20]

In phase one, look beyond just the people with whom you work regularly. I love meeting new people at conferences, seminars, workshops, and symposiums. Outside of work, friends, family members, classmates from school, or even folks from volunteer events are worth considering. New networks are also great places to search. These can include rotary clubs, Vistage (an executive coaching organization), your local Chamber of Commerce, or industry-specific groups like the Society for Human Resource Management, Project Management Institute, Armed Forces Communications & Electronics Association, or CONNECTpreneur (all groups I mined for board members throughout my career).

Leveraging Technology

Technology and digital platforms can help in many phases of the connection, networking, and relationship-building process. However, it's *not* OK to just "sprinkle on some tech" and call it a day. We need to first learn; figure out what works best for each of us; and then see where tech can help us save time, reduce error, and streamline processes. LinkedIn is a great place to do initial, larger-scale screenings and searches. You can also ask for referrals from existing board members.

Tips for Networking (Meeting New People)

"Your network is your net worth."

Unknown (I did not come up with this gem myself!)

---

20 Hill, L. and K. Linebeck. (2011). "The Three Networks You Need." *Harvard Business Review.* https://hbr.org/2011/03/the-three-networks-you-need.

When you're meeting new people, make sure that you have time and capacity to give your full attention to the other person you are meeting, whether in person, on a video call, or while messaging in online communities. When meeting in person, eye contact is huge, and being fully present will quickly build the foundation of trust before you even make an ask. (There's a great book by Casey McEwen on this.)

The list of networking tricks below came from one of the most "networked" or connected people that I know. He suggests

- always arriving early to networking events
- offer to help as an impromptu volunteer if you arrive early
- ask for a copy of the guest list in advance of the event to better prepare by planning to have a few people in mind who you are hoping to meet
- look at the check-in table with name badges to see who has not yet arrived
- start your mingling in the bar line or the food line (you do not need to order an alcoholic drink at events; often I will order a seltzer with lime, and nobody knows the difference)
- ask the bartender what kind of drinks they like to make and try something new—your drink is another conversation starter!

If you are at a networking event with vendors and booths, it's also a great starting point to walk from booth to booth and learn about the offerings from each of the vendors. Even if you are not their ideal customer, you can let them know that you are new to this and are willing to help send the right prospects their way as you mingle more; I have yet to meet somebody who turns down free business development and marketing.

What follows is a list of other questions to consider asking at in-person networking events to get the conversation flowing:

1. *What brought you to this event?*
2. *What are you looking to gain from this event—what would be an awesome outcome for you?*
3. *What initially drew you to your current profession/industry?*
4. *How do you stay up-to-date with current events and industry trends?*
5. *What's the most exciting project you're currently working on?*
6. *Can you recommend any professional development resources? What books are you reading?*

7. How do you maintain work-life balance in this busy profession?
8. What advice would you give to someone new to your industry?
9. What's one challenge in your field that you would like to solve?
10. Who inspires you professionally?
11. If you could go back in your career, is there anything you'd do differently?
12. Have you seen [NAME from the guest list]? I would love to say hello and meet them. (Warm referrals can also work on the spot!)

Bonus tip from professional speaker Conor Neill: if you can start off with, "I think we know somebody in common," it makes it very difficult for them to walk away without hearing a little more.

Remember, the other people at the event are also there to network. In fact, walking up to tables or small groups and saying, "Hey, do you mind if I join you? I'm looking to meet new people," has never failed me. Doing it with a smile on your face helps a lot. Your goal is to make new connections. People love talking about themselves, so let them talk! A great sign of a superb networker is someone who can balance building trust and rapport, asking questions, and sharing their story, all while making you feel like their top priority in a matter of minutes.

Remember to "read the room" as you're conversing. If you start to ramble or dive deep into a topic that doesn't interest the other person, you may see them check the time, yawn, look at their watch or phone, ask fewer questions, or lose focused eye contact. This might mean it's time to ask them about their work or pose a non-yes/no question. Remember: you have two ears but only one mouth for a reason!

I recently acquired a valuable skill from a Dale Carnegie class on meeting new people and establishing initial rapport. Figure 25 elaborates on some of the concepts I absorbed from the class. Review the easy-to-remember, fun conversation pieces on the left side of the image, and see if you can incorporate them into your next networking event to gather insights from the "Learning Concept" column—the aspects we genuinely want to discover about others.

Dale Carnegie was an American writer, lecturer, and developer of courses in self-improvement, salesmanship, corporate training, public speaking, and interpersonal skills. Born into modest circumstances in Missouri, he became a sought-after speaker and trainer in the early twentieth century. His most famous work, *How to Win Friends and Influence People* (published in 1936), remains one of the best-selling books of all time and is foundational to his training programs.

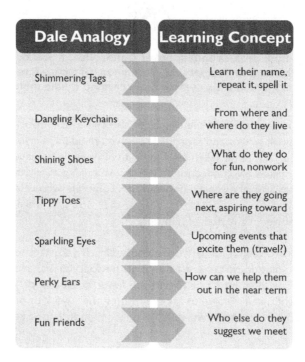

Dale Analogy	Learning Concept
Shimmering Tags	Learn their name, repeat it, spell it
Dangling Keychains	From where and where do they live
Shining Shoes	What do they do for fun, nonwork
Tippy Toes	Where are they going next, aspiring toward
Sparkling Eyes	Upcoming events that excite them (travel?)
Perky Ears	How can we help them out in the near term
Fun Friends	Who else do they suggest we meet

Figure 25: This graphic builds on concepts that I learned from a class focused on meeting new people and building an initial rapport.

Let's assume you hit it off in the initial meeting and asked to schedule a follow-up call to get to know this person a little better. The goal of that call is to learn more about their background and get a feel for their goals, see how they align with yours, and determine if you actually like one another! You don't have to jump right into reciting your résumé or LinkedIn profile to them. What if you shared something interesting about your childhood and how it influenced where you are today? And maybe next, discuss what you do for fun on Sundays. Curveballs in networking set you apart and generate interest. If there's a professional spark, then it makes sense to keep progressing.

Introvert in the Networking Game

Introverts are individuals who often feel more comfortable or recharged in solitary or low-stimulus environments, versus extroverts, who typically thrive and gain energy from social interactions. (However, introversion and extroversion exist on a spectrum, with many people identifying as "ambiverts"—those who display traits of both personality types.) Despite these differences, introverts need not feel excluded from the world of networking. Virtual networking offers a space where introverts can initiate and build relationships at their own pace, without the immediate pressure of face-to-face interactions. Platforms like LinkedIn or specialized forums allow for thoughtful exchanges, providing ample time to craft responses. Furthermore, smaller niche events or workshops, both online and offline, cater to an introvert's preference for in-depth, one-on-one conversations. Networking isn't solely about quantity; for many, the depth and quality of connections can hold far more value.

Networking Personas

As you embark on the networking journey, envision it as setting sail on expansive waters, where every interaction is with another sailor, also in an exploratory journey of their own.

First, there's the Exploratory Seeker. Always on the lookout for new horizons, they're brimming with curiosity. Their open-minded approach is refreshing, allowing for diverse conversations. However, their broad interests might sometimes make it hard to find an anchor for focused dialogue.

Then, you'll encounter the Expert. With a wealth of experience, they are a seasoned navigator of these waters. Their in-depth knowledge is a compass for many; yet sometimes their vast expertise can overshadow other voices, turning discussions into monologues.

Making waves is the Energetic Superconnector. They seem to know every sailor in the sea and are always keen to make introductions. Their vast network can open up new routes and opportunities, but their rapid pace might sometimes feel overwhelming if you're seeking a more in-depth connection. These are great people to hang out with (if you can handle them) at networking events.

Not far off is the Newcomer. Their vessel might be new to these waters, but their enthusiasm is contagious. Their fresh perspectives can be invigorating, but they might occasionally need a guiding star to help them navigate the networking seas.

Quietly charting their course is the Observer. They listen more than they speak, absorbing the ebb and flow around them. Engaging with them can lead to insightful exchanges, but you might often need to initiate the conversation.

Sailing with a relaxed confidence is the Chill Veteran. With many voyages behind them, they approach networking with ease. Their stories are both enlightening and entertaining, but they might sometimes stick to familiar routes and appear hesitant to explore new waters. This is another great person to hang out with at networking events if the Energetic Superconnector is too much for you.

On a clear course is the Transactional Salesperson. They know what they seek and are direct in their approach. Their clarity can lead to fruitful collaborations, but their focus on transactions might lack the warmth of genuine relationship-building.

Lastly, there's the Wallflower. Often overlooked, they carry a wealth of deep insights. Venturing toward them can be rewarding, but it might take an extra effort to start the exchange.

As you navigate these waters, recognize that these personas can help you set the right course, ensuring a journey filled with meaningful connections and valuable insights.

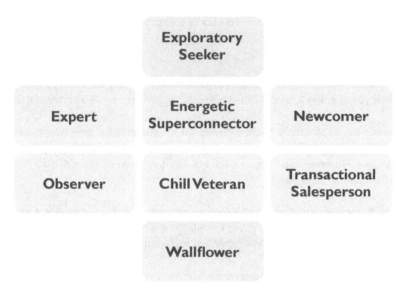

Figure 26: The personas you may come across at a typical (large) professional networking event. Ideally, you are spending the most time with the two innermost personas.

What Not to Do When Reaching Out to People

Never run right up and tell someone what you need from them! Think of how rude and transactional it would seem if someone did that to you. When initially meeting somebody or asking somebody on a date, do you immediately ask them to become your significant other in the next few moments? I bet you instead take a less intrusive approach and get a feel for one another to see if you are even compatible as people first.

Each relationship with a prospective board member can be correlated to dating. It is unlikely that you'll get married after the first date, and it is equally unlikely that you'll fill a board seat after your initial interaction with an individual. It is also true that not all people are a good fit for one another. Again, this is totally fine. You can genuinely appreciate people and the work that they do, but at the end of the day, you may not be a good fit for one another—just like dating. Do not settle for "*a* mentor" while in search of "*the* mentor" for your personal board. I've learned many times that the wrong person in a role—at work or on a personal board—can be far worse than no person in that slot.

There's a story I often think of when I need to be reminded of the power of persistence. A Supervisor of mine and a Buddy on my board suggested that I reach out to a big-time mover and shaker in our organization who belonged to another team. Both board members "just knew" that this other person— we will call her Allison—and I would hit it off and feed off one another's energy. She had been in my role before; we'd both gone through the same leadership development program; and we both loved to travel, play basketball, and meet new people. Safe to say I was excited—but this is where things went south. I sent an email to her, making it clear that our common connections had suggested a conversation and coffee. I followed up a week later, then a month later—no response. I was able to find her work phone number and left a voicemail after the one-week email and again after three weeks. I also asked another person to do a text intro for us. After six weeks, I was just about done trying. The very next day, Allison arrived at my cubicle, coffee in hand. "Hey," she said, "I heard you were trying to reach me while I was out on maternity leave. You up for a coffee chat?" The persistence paid off, and she actually thanked me for not giving up.

Most professionals will overtly tell you to stop the outreach and follow-up if they truly do not have time—so until you get an answer (even a "no"), it pays to be persistent. Don't be rude and don't overdo the follow-up, but if you don't hear back right away, there might be a reason that has nothing to do with you! (And yes, "Allison" did join my PBA for about eight months while I grew in my program management position, and we stayed in touch after I left that team and that company.)

Throughout this chapter, we've journeyed through the art of networking and the significance of forging meaningful connections. Each interaction, each story shared, and each lesson learned paves the way for deeper, more genuine relationships. But remember, meeting the right people is just the beginning. Knowing how to build and nurture relationships is the foundation; however, the real magic happens when we channel these connections purposefully.

As we turn the page, we're poised to take the next crucial step: constructing your personal board. This isn't just about gathering names but about curating a group of individuals who will be instrumental in guiding, challenging, and supporting you in your endeavors. Armed with the knowledge from this chapter, you're now ready to start filling your board with the right people. Onward to the next chapter, where we delve into the intricacies of building a robust and influential personal board!

Action and Reflection

As we wrap up Chapter 6, start to think about which of these tips and tricks you may try out next!

1. Is it time for you to find a new networking event to attend this month?

2. If you haven't already, write down a list of the people in each of your needed networks: (1) operational (people you interact with daily), (2) developmental (people you trust and turn to for advice), and (3) strategic (people who help you plan for the future).

3. Which networking tip will you try out at the next networking event you attend?

4. Which networking persona are you? The Exploratory Seeker, Expert, Energetic Superconnector, Newcomer, Observer, Chill Veteran, Transactional Salesperson, or the Wallflower?

5. Think about what you do after you make a connection with somebody at a networking event or on LinkedIn. What are the follow-up steps you take? Are they working? Could you do something better or more effectively?

Space for your notes and reflection.

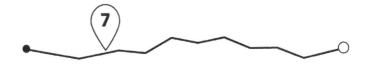

CHAPTER 7

BOARD-BUILDING PROCESS

"The strength of the team is each individual member. The strength of each member is the team."

Phil Jackson, the master of the hardwood, coaching his basketball teams to championship nirvana with his unique coaching philosophy

This chapter takes the networking concepts from the last chapter and focuses on driving outreach to build your personal board. We will walk through the strategic steps involved in constructing your personal board, discussing the significance of each role in shaping your career map and selecting the right individuals for each role. By intentionally choosing advisors who align with your values and aspirations, you can tap into a wealth of knowledge, guidance, and support that will propel you toward your goals. When you finish this chapter, you will understand what kinds of people you may want on your board, how to contact them, and, once you have the introductory call scheduled, how to prepare for the first session (more on the conversation flow in Chapter 10).

From Networking to Board-Building

You may realize that there are already many people in your life who could fill some of your board seats, but you might not have someone in mind for every role. Here are three key areas where you may find potential board members:

Existing Ties: Recognize the potential mentors already in your life. Whether from college, previous jobs, or other circles, these connections often form the foundation of your board.

Strategic Outreach: Leverage the networking techniques from the last chapter to intentionally cultivate new relationships.

Professional Platforms: Engage in industry events, online forums, and associations. Such platforms are gold mines for potential board members.

Personal Connections and Referrals

Personal connections can often lead to the most meaningful and productive board relationships. Seek recommendations from trusted individuals who can vouch for the expertise and credibility of potential board members—and for you.

Before I started my first job in supply chain, I experimented with the concept of a referral by asking my supervisor for a name or two of someone who could help me prepare to hit the ground running. Matt, my soon-to-be boss, knew a little about me and, more importantly, understood the work that I would be doing. So, he managed to do some matching magic to find two people who aligned with my planned work, my background, and my personality. These "pre-Buddy" referral conversations were extremely helpful, and one of the individuals ended up sitting on my PBA as a functional mentor for the next twelve months! It never hurts to ask for a referral.

Building Your Personal Board: Implementation Planning

Once you've identified potential board members, develop an implementation plan with clear steps and timelines for engaging them. Think about your onboarding and orientation process with each board member—perhaps you will have a few things you share with them in advance and some baseline questions that you ask when getting started. Prep work goes a long way in showing them that you are taking this seriously and that you appreciate their time.

Let's assume the first meeting is scheduled and you have a calendar invite with their email address in it. You also know their full name, so you can begin to do a little research!

Start by giving yourself a LinkedIn refresher (after you ensure you're connected, of course). What are they posting about? What kinds of posts are they liking and commenting on? What are their skills, interests, volunteering positions, work and education history, etc.? Do you share any mutual connections?

Next, Google their name and company to see if you can understand what they do. I felt quite silly while at a dinner with a potential mentor when he asked me if I had any idea what his company did. I totally botched it and, instead of saying, "No, I did not take time to look at that," I tried to piece together some baloney. Bad idea. Please learn from my mistake!

After you've done your due diligence on them, you can make their due diligence easy by emailing or texting a thirty-second selfie video where you share:

- Your "why" and purpose
- What you do for fun (outside of work)
- What you've done before professionally
- What you are doing now professionally
- What do you wish to do next professionally (and why)

Sharing your résumé (or a draft of your career map!) can be helpful as well, but I suggest holding off on doing this until after your first conversation so you can get a feel for whether they are indeed interested in growing together. This may also be a good follow-up action after your first conversation.

Establishing the Order of Building Your Personal Board

There is no set timeline for fully building out your board. In my experience, it seems that giving yourself a full year is a reasonable timeframe for getting started with an entirely empty board. On the other hand, you may be able to fill out your board in fifteen minutes. Remember that it is not one-size-fits-all. If you already have your full board developed, then the following sections may help you review and perhaps refresh some of the members on your board. If you are just getting started, it may be valuable to review the professional development journey process flow in Figure 27. This builds on the ikigai concepts and the start of your career map to methodically plan out where you have support and clearly identify the gaps in your PBA.

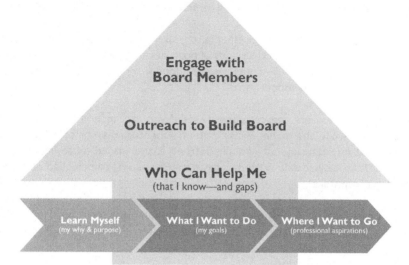

Figure 27: Overview of the professional development journey process flow starting with learning about yourself to the ongoing stage of engaging with members on your PBA

The companion website has a professional development journey worksheet that aligns with Figure 27. I use this worksheet with students and early career professionals often. It has also helped many mid-career employees as a refresher!

What follows is my suggested order to build a PBA. Note that this does not mean you necessarily have to start from the top of this list, nor do you have to start on the left-hand side of this plot. This is a guide for those just getting started, whereas you may be further along and ready to move board seats around (which is very OK to do). See what you can fill out on your board from this section!

Start with your **Buddy: The Peer Support Advisor:** Develop relationships with peers or colleagues who can serve as accountability partners, sounding boards, and sources of feedback and collaboration.

Next is the **Functional Mentor: The Experienced Guide and Inside Advisor:** Find an experienced and trusted mentor who can provide guidance, share knowledge, and offer valuable insights based on their expertise and experience.

With your **Supervisor/Manager: The Professional Supervisor and Tactical Advisor:** Engage with your current or previous boss as a board member to gain insights, feedback, and guidance specific to your role and organizational dynamics.

Note: If you are working at a company, you will likely be assigned a boss or a supervisor—so start there, then find a Buddy and a Functional Mentor. If you are your own boss, you may not have this "boss" seat to fill at all, so you might want to jump straight to finding a Functional Mentor. If you are earlier in your career, it may make sense to prioritize the Buddy. Many companies assign a Buddy (who may not be the best fit initially), and they may even assign a mentor. If you are starting this journey with an established career, you may look for a Mentee and/or Functional Mentor to fill your first board seats.

In the next six months of your career-mapping journey, find your **Champion: The Strategic Guidance and "Split-Level" Support Advisor:** Identify someone who believes in your potential, supports your goals, and advocates for your success. A Champion can provide encouragement and help open doors to opportunities. Then, find your **Cross-Functional Mentor: The Specialist Mentor and Outside Advisor,** and your **Accountability Partner: The Responsible Advisor.**

In the final three months of your first year on this journey, identify an **Ally: The Collaborative Supporting Partner and Perspective Advisor:** Seek an ally who understands your gaps and challenges; shares similar values; and can provide emotional support, encouragement, and a safe space for discussions. Also, look for a **Sponsor: The Influential Advocate and Background Advisor** who has influence and can actively advocate for your career advancement, recommend you for promotions or important projects, and help raise your professional profile.

In years two to ten, you can start to pay it forward and help others, i.e., your **Mentee** (someone you mentor) and your **Successor** (the person you think will be the successor in a specific role). As a reminder: just because I'm suggesting your mentor be five to ten years ahead of you doesn't mean you have to wait that long to start mentoring others.

In years five to fifteen, you'll likely benefit from having a **Coach: The Project-Based Tactical Advisor.**

After more than fifteen years, it's time to find a **Successor: The Protégé-in-Training and Reverse Mentor,** and learn how to be a good successee and reverse mentor. As you progress in your career, consider identifying a potential successor who can learn from you, take on responsibilities, and eventually step into your role.

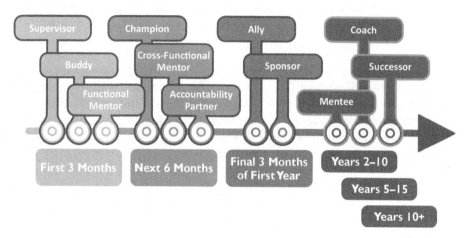

Figure 28: Sample process flow for how you may go about building out a PBA in a twelve-month cycle. This can be condensed if certain pieces are already in place for your board!

A common question I get asked on this topic is, "Do I actually need to call these helpers 'mentors,' and do they have to know that they are formally on my personal board?" My short answer is no; you do not have to make this overly formal every time, as long as you are tracking your PBA in some manner. My longer response is that it depends. I personally prefer to thank them for acting in a mentoring function or for being a Sponsor. I do think it is important to let others know in some way that you are learning from them and that their guidance over time is valuable. The concern with making the relationship overly formal is that some people get scared off by these kinds of commitments. I've observed dozens of successful mentoring relationships where the mentee does not formally award the title/position of Functional Mentor. Another option is to take a somewhat jocular approach to this and ask them if they are ready to "DTR: define the relationship."

Action and Reflection

As we wrap up Chapter 7, start to think about who is in your network now and who has been guiding you thus far on your professional voyage.

1. Who in your network may already be on your PBA?

2. Which board seat do you plan to fill next?

3. Could you ask one of your current board members for a warm referral or introduction to a prospect that could fill a current or soon-to-be-open board seat?

4. Would it be valuable for you to offer to make a warm referral for someone on your personal board to help them with their board-building process? It's not just one-way with these relationships!

Space for your notes and reflection.

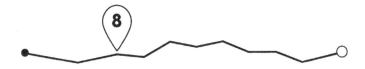

CHAPTER 8

THE "-IRING" PROCESS(ES)

HIRING, FIRING, RETIRING, AND REWIRING YOUR BOARD

"Sometimes letting things go is an act of far greater power than defending or hanging on."

Eckhart Tolle, a German writer and speaker, who covered many broad topics related to philosophical and spiritual influences, including in his book The Power of Now

This short chapter on the "-iring" process(es), pronounced "eye-ring" will guide you through the necessary steps to make changes to your board when required, ensuring that it continues to serve your evolving needs and aspirations.

Identifying When Changes Are Needed

Changes to your personal board may be necessitated by various factors, including:

- Achieving specific career milestones and reassessing goals
- Shifting career directions or exploring new opportunities
- Changes in the availability or expertise of your board members

Figure 29 is likely one that you can relate to. We plan for one particular path and set of events but rarely do things ever go entirely as planned. The arrow on the left represents what we plan for and expect. The curvy, squiggly arrow on the right shows what I have found to be a much more realistic journey through the professional world. This is why we give ourselves flexibility and bring stability to the PBA!

Planned Career   Actual Career

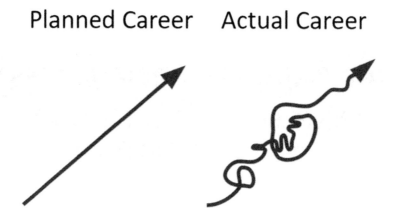

Figure 29: Compare the straight line of a planned career to the curvy line representing our actual career journey full of twists and turns and loops.

Recognizing when changes are needed is the first step toward maintaining a dynamic and effective personal board. The following process, inspired by the Agile methodology, is one that I have followed over the last decade when handling my own PBA and supporting the development of personal boards of others.

1. **Desire** - Determine what you really want and need.
2. **Inquire** - See who is out there.
3. **Hire** - Formally onboard them and start connecting.
4. **Admire** - Say "thank you" and appreciate the progress made.
5. **Fire** - They're no longer a good fit, "let's end this now."
6. **Retire** - Recognize you grew out of a need.
7. **Rewire** - Think of who else needs to be on your board.
8. **Inspire** - Brainstorm whose board can you now be on.

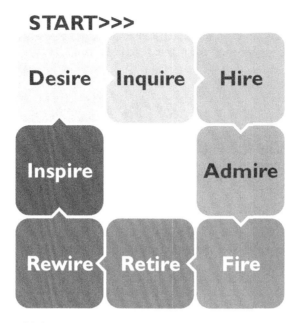

START>>>

Desire Inquire Hire

Inspire Admire

Rewire Retire Fire

Figure 30: Outlines the "iring" process(es) to follow when building out your PBA.

Desire

The process starts with some searching inside of yourself! We talked about your why and ikigai—this is step one. What is it that you really want and need for yourself? With these answers in hand, you can begin to determine which board seats are already filled and which seats need to be filled next. You can start to think about what you want to accomplish with each board member, aligning with your SMARTY goals.

Inquire

Building on the concepts from recent chapters, this is where you see who is out there! Seek warm referrals from existing board members and your current professional network.

I am in no way saying that you should be coy about approaching a personal board member to set up some one-on-one time but do be cognizant and respectful of their time and attention. You can always supplement in between direct interactions through passive learning—i.e., the ability, honed over time, to absorb knowledge, insights, and wisdom from your mentors without constantly seeking their attention or guidance. This can be achieved by observing their actions, listening attentively during discussions, studying their decision-making processes, and analyzing their strategies.

For instance, in addition to frequently asking direct questions, learn by observing your board members' problem-solving methods. If applicable, read materials they've recommended or even authored. Attend meetings or presentations where they're speaking, if possible. This way, you're learning from them indirectly without always requiring their direct involvement.

When you meet with them, share your proposed goals and expectations, roles, and responsibilities as the situation warrants. (Remember that not every person you query will be a great fit for your board! You may have to keep "dating" to find the right person.)

More on where to find people and how to ask prospective board members to join your board was covered in Chapter 6.

Hire

"Hiring" involves formally onboarding individuals to your board and kicking off conversations. Chapter 9 dives deep into what each of the conversations will look like when getting started.

We will pick back up with the rest of the -iring process in Part III after we dive into what to do with each of the board members. A reminder that the remaining pieces are:

4. **Admire - Say "thank you" and appreciate the progress made.**

5. **Fire - They're no longer a good fit, "let's end this now."**

6. **Retire - Recognize you grew out of a need.**

7. **Rewire - Think of who else needs to be on your board.**

8. **Inspire - Brainstorm whose board can you now be on.**

Action and Reflection

As we wrap up Chapter 8, start to think about the phases of the "-iring" process that you have already started with your own PBA.

1. Do you need to start thinking about swapping in/out any current mentors? Are they still aligned with your SMARTY goals?

2. Is there a need to change the way you have been engaging with your mentors?

3. Are you ready to "hire" your next board member today? This week? This month?

Space for your notes and reflection.

PART

ENGAGING WITH YOUR PERSONAL BOARD OF ADVISORS

The following chapters will cover the roles, responsibilities, goals, and expectations for you and the other members on your personal board. Part II touches on a few of the questions to ask each person and how often to engage with them. I encourage you to read a little, then act by updating your PBA (on the companion website or a worksheet) while refining your career map along the way.

Each chapter about a board member will walk through the following;

1. Years of experience
2. Internal versus external (to your organization)
3. Goals for the relationship
4. Career map contributions
5. The board member's background and where you found them
6. Frequency of interactions and conversations over time
7. Conversation flow and any details that differ from Chapter 9
8. What to avoid
9. What to do when you are filling this board seat for others
10. Action and reflection (like we do for every chapter!)

	Ch.	Experience	Internal vs External	Your Goal with Them	Career Map Focus	Their Background (found where)	Meeting Frequency (over time)
Buddy	10						
Accountability Partner	11						
Functional Mentor	12						
Cross-Functional Mentor	13						
Coach	14						
Sponsor	15						
Champion	16						
Ally	17						
Supervisor/ Manager	18						
Successor	19						

Figure 31: Sample of the reference template table AKA "The PBA Matrix" that we will fill in at the end of each PBA seat chapter in Part II.

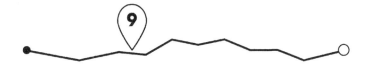

CHAPTER 9:

CONVO PREP AND BOARDS GONE WRONG

"Tell me and I forget, teach me and I may remember, involve me and I learn."

Benjamin Franklin, electric inventor who "shocked" the world with his wit, wisdom, and a kite-flying experiment that truly "sparked" curiosity

After diligently building your PBA in Part I, the journey enters its next phase: engagement. This chapter offers a blueprint for nurturing these pivotal relationships, ensuring you derive maximum value while avoiding common pitfalls.

Phases of PBA Planning

We are going to think like a systems engineer with an agile, human-centric design approach. If you're not an engineer (or not an engineer *yet*), that's okay; this simply means that we are going to structure the thinking a bit.

Think of this as a "plan, do, check, act, iterate" process:

Plan out what you need from a specific board member professionally, namely where they may be able to help answer questions or fill gaps in your career map. It's a great conversation to bring up one or two questions! A board member typically has more experience than you for a reason, and it is OK to be clear that you do not have all the answers.

Do the first phase of career mapping on your own, and then share it with your Buddy for some feedback to see if it makes sense. Is there anything that you missed? Offer to be a second set of eyes for their map too! Remember, the elements you're looking for are: what you did, where you are, and where you want to go (with a few backup options at each stage).

Check on the progress of your career map throughout each year. I typically add a quarterly reminder on my calendar. It is helpful to look at your career map with each member of your board at least two times annually.

Act—Go get your work done and keep working toward your destination. (Keep it simple!)

Iterate—If at first you do not succeed in achieving your goals, then tweak the *plan-do-check-act* process and go again!

Board Conversation Flow

Engaging with your board members requires a structured approach. While the following chapters delve into specifics for each board member, this chapter outlines a general conversation flow for all your professional development interactions.

Aim for discussions lasting between thirty and sixty minutes. Especially early in the relationship, longer conversations can be more beneficial.

This guide serves as a flexible roadmap. Your conversations might progress differently, and that's okay. The key is to maintain the essence of each discussion.

Conversation 1: Laying the Foundation

After the discovery call, this first development conversation sets the stage for how this relationship will progress.

- Background Sharing: Dive into both of your professional histories. Discuss what you enjoyed, what you found challenging, and what came naturally.

- Driving Forces: Share your motivations and purpose. Why are you on this path?

- Personal Insights: Discuss hobbies and interests. Building rapport is essential, especially early on.

- Future Aspirations: Highlight your professional goals. Why are they important to you?

- Commitment: Pledge to partner for at least one year, ideally with monthly meetings. As comfort grows, consider holding them every two months.

- Cadence and Communication: Agree on meeting regularity and preferred communication modes. Set up the next few meetings.

"Success is a journey, not a destination. The doing is often more important than the outcome."

Arthur Ashe, an American tennis player, and civil rights activist who was known for his talent on the court and his commitment to social justice

Make sure that you have enough time to actually invest in this relationship with this board member. Make sure they have the time as well. This is something that you can clarify and confirm during your orientation session with the new board member.

Conversation 2: Setting Expectations and Goals

- Communication Preferences: Understand each other's communication styles and preferences. Confirm their ongoing preferred method of communication: Zoom/Teams/Facetime (video call), phone call, text, in-person coffee, or something else. Are there any they actively dislike?

- Goal Setting: Define your relationship's objectives. Schedule quarterly reviews.

- Career Mapping: Outline your career trajectory, discussing past hurdles and potential growth opportunities.

- Learning from the Past: Discuss beneficial aspects of previous mentoring relationships.

- Boundaries: Highlight off-limits topics, ensuring clear lines of communication.

Conversation 3: Looking Ahead

- Career Milestones: Discuss pivotal moments and achievements to aim for.

- Anticipating Challenges: Explore potential roadblocks in your current role.

- Growth Opportunities: Identify stretch assignments and experiences to seek.

- Skillsets and Experiences: Discuss specific areas to focus on for career advancement.

- Feedback Loop: Regularly check if your expectations align with your goals. This continual feedback ensures both parties remain on track.

- Appreciation: Ask how they like to be thanked and what you could perhaps do for them.

Subsequent and Impromptu Conversations

- Reviewing Actions: Discuss progress and practical applications of previous discussions.
- Overcoming Hurdles: If you stumble, how can you regain confidence? Celebrate small victories to boost morale.
- Celebrations: Acknowledge achievements. Consider creating a "rewards list" to celebrate milestones.
- Networking: Seek recommendations for other professionals with whom you might engage.
- Open Board Seats: Discuss any vacancies in each other's boards.
- Career Map Review: Periodically revisit your career map, identifying progress and areas of focus.

Structuring Individual Board Conversations

When engaging in a conversation with a member of your PBA, it's crucial to approach it in stages: before, during, and after the conversation. Each stage has its own set of tasks and considerations to ensure a productive and respectful exchange. Note that the flow of conversation with each board member will have some similarities and will begin to vary as each relationship matures and builds.

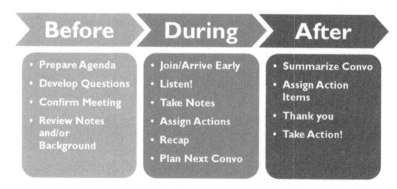

Figure 32: Outline of the before, during, and after conversation flow to follow with each member of your PBA.

Before the Conversation

Preparation is key. Start by creating an agenda for the meeting, outlining the topics you wish to discuss. This should be shared with your board member twenty-four hours in advance as part of a reminder and confirmation email, which should also include the location of the meeting whether it's in person or virtual. The agenda should also include a few questions you'd like to discuss, which provides the board member with a chance to prepare their thoughts. Review notes from any previous conversations and provide a status update on any action items, if applicable. Lastly, review their background to refresh your memory and ensure you're fully prepared for the conversation. You can also take a few moments to refresh or reflect on what you bring to your relationships with mentors and advisors. Consider the value you can offer them in return for their support. Explore ways to provide mutual benefits and create a symbiotic relationship.

During the Conversation

Join the meeting two or three minutes early as a courtesy, especially if the meeting is in person. This shows respect for your board member's time. Take notes during the meeting to reduce unnecessary interruptions. Listen attentively, be present, and assign action items. Remember to respect their time and end the meeting on time. (If you need to go over the allotted time, ask in advance if they can spare an additional ten minutes.) Finish by planning the next call, including the date, location, and a high-level overview of the agenda.

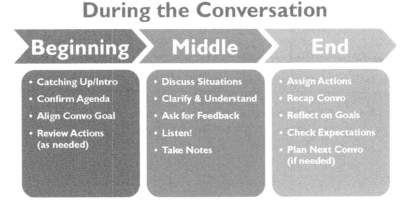

Figure 33: Conversation flow that you can build off of for each conversation, outlining the beginning, the middle, and the end of the conversation.

Asking for feedback during conversations with your PBA is a critical step towards continued growth and development. Chapter 20 will go into more detail about the feedback process. I know you do not want to wait for the juicy details, so the following four-step process will have to hold you over until Part III. A simple way to go "Ask for Feedback" is to ask one another: What should I start doing? What should I stop doing? What should I continue doing? What should I shift the way I am doing it?

We Ask Them

What should I **start** doing?
What should I **stop** doing?
What should I **continue** doing?
What should I **shift** the way I am doing it?

They Ask Us

Figure 34: The start-stop-continue-shift feedback methodology that I like to use for feedback conversations and one-on-one check-ins.

After the Conversation

Follow up with an email summarizing the talking points discussed, sharing action items (what to do, who owns it, and estimated completion date), and expressing your gratitude for their time. Send the calendar invitation for the next meeting if you haven't already done so. Start to complete your actions and make progress.

One of the most powerful "after the conversation" experiences of my life came about ten months after a series of conversations with Tony, a friend of my brother and (as I realized later) one of my first professional mentees. He called me and thanked me a lot for the time I spent with him, the insights I shared, the connections I made, and the questions I helped him think through. He shared that these chats changed his life (wow!). Our time together helped him rethink his professional career and set him up for big time success. He went from getting ready to start a job to pay the bills to pursuing grad school and accepting a position that he loved and was far more excited about. We were in totally different industries, and all I did was help him see things a bit differently and ask a few questions. These are the kinds of moments that fuel me and make me jump out of bed in the morning!

DTR: Defining (and Formalizing) The Relationship

It is very helpful to agree on the goals and expectations at the beginning of a PBA relationship, and I've seen many mentoring programs issue a "mentorship agreement" that both the mentor and mentee need to sign. As mentioned earlier, this level of formality is not required for every single member of your board, but it is a nice way to add structure, rigor, and formality to the key strategic people on your PBA.

A mutual development agreement (MDA) is a structured way to lay the groundwork for a mentor/mentee relationship. At the core of the MDA is the Purpose and Objectives section, which establishes why the parties are entering into this agreement and the goals they hope to achieve. The Duration of the agreement should be specified, whether it's for a fixed period or open-ended with scheduled reviews.

Key to the relationship are the roles and responsibilities of each party. The mentee might be responsible for regular updates, preparing for meetings, and being receptive to feedback. On the other hand, the mentor might commit to attending regular check-ins, offering specific guidance, and providing relevant resources. The frequency of interactions and the preferred method of communication (such as email, phone, or in-person meetings) should be outlined to maintain regular touchpoints.

Confidentiality is paramount, especially when business-sensitive topics are at play, so both parties should commit to keeping their discussions private. If business-sensitive information is involved, noncompete/nonsolicit clauses may be necessary to safeguard against potential conflicts of interest. A conflict resolution mechanism can preemptively address potential disagreements or misunderstandings. Furthermore, a feedback mechanism ensures that both the mentor and mentee can openly share their perspectives and grow from the experience.

As the relationship progresses, it's beneficial to schedule times to Review and Revise the MDA to ensure its continued relevance. While this is typically an agreement based on mutual trust, having both parties sign the MDA can instill a sense of commitment and seriousness. Any Compensation or exchange of services should be detailed, even if the relationship is not monetarily based. Lastly, it's important to clarify that the MDA does not entail any legal obligations and is simply a guide based on mutual respect and trust.

Sample Mutual Development Agreement (MDA)

Between:
Mentee: Alex Rodriguez, Senior Sales Representative at Lattitude
Mentor: Jordan Smith, Sales Director at Lattitude

1. **Purpose and Objectives:**
   This agreement seeks to foster professional growth for Alex Rodriguez in his role as a Senior Sales Representative. The primary goals include enhancing sales techniques, understanding advanced sales strategies, and building a robust network within the industry.

2. **Duration:**
   This agreement will span twelve months from the date of signing, with a review at the end of this period.

3. **Roles and Responsibilities:**
   Mentee (Alex): Alex commits to providing monthly updates on sales performance, preparing ahead of each meeting, and actively seeking and implementing feedback.

   Mentor (Jordan): Jordan will offer guidance on advanced sales techniques, provide relevant resources, and facilitate introductions to key industry figures.

4. **Frequency of Interactions:**
   The pair will meet biweekly, with ad hoc meetings as necessary.

5. **Method of Communication:**
   Primary communication will be virtual meetings with at least one in-person meeting, with email for follow-ups and scheduling.

6. **Confidentiality:**
   Both parties pledge to keep all discussions and shared information confidential.

7. **Feedback Mechanism:**
   Feedback will be provided at the end of each meeting, with a more comprehensive review every three months.

8. **Termination:**
   This agreement can be terminated by either party with fifteen days' notice.

9. **Compensation:**
   This mentorship is based on mutual professional growth and does not involve monetary compensation.

10. **Noncompete/Nonsolicit Clauses:**
    Both parties agree not to use the information discussed for competing purposes or solicit each other's clients or contacts without prior permission.

11. **Review and Revisions:**
    The MDA will be reviewed at the three-month mark to ensure its continued relevance.

12. **Signatures:**

Note: This MDA is based on mutual trust and respect and does not create any legal obligations or liabilities for either party.

Alex Rodriguez, Senior Sales Rep: _____ Date: _____

Jordan Smith, Sales Director: _____ Date: _____

A template of this agreement (MDA) is available on the companion website.

Boards Gone Wrong—What to Avoid and What Not to Do

"And the man in the back said everyone attack and it turned into a ballroom blitz"

The Sweet, band with this iconic line that rocked the music scene with their glam rock anthems in the 1970s

One Person, Two Board Seats

One of the top questions I get asked when speaking and presenting on the topic of PBAs revolves around one person filling multiple board seats. My answer is that it's best and most ideal to find one unique individual for each board seat. Think about their primary purpose in guiding you on your professional development journey. A Cross-Functional Mentor can also act as a Champion, but be clear about the main focus when building out your PBA. Early in your career, it is likely that your Supervisor and/or Buddy will also be a Functional Mentor to you. Great. But what happens if you leave that company? You'll have no more boss and perhaps no more mentor—meaning you have two open seats to fill now. Consider if you had an Ally who was also your Sponsor and Champion, and in one month, that person gets removed from your board. That's almost 38 percent of your board gone! The goal is to eliminate single points of failure. (I never said this would be easy!)

Multiple Seats of the Same Role (e.g., Three Buddies)

At certain points in our careers, we may have an expanded board that includes multiple Buddies or more than one Functional Mentor. That's fine. You have read multiple stories about my experiences with more than one Functional Mentor and more than one Champion, Sponsor, etc. The purpose of this book is for you to find the most ideal, primary person to fill each of your board seats, and then you can certainly go on to add multiple Functional Mentors, Allies, Buddies, and more. Hopefully, you don't have to add too many Supervisors/Managers!

Establishing and Maintaining Communication Boundaries

How can you ensure effective and productive interactions with your PBA?

The key lies in establishing and maintaining appropriate communication boundaries. This involves emphasizing professionalism and discretion when engaging with board members. It's crucial to avoid discussing sensitive personal matters that do not contribute to professional growth. Similarly, refrain from seeking personal advice that falls outside the realm of professional development. Be mindful not to overshare personal details that exceed the scope of professional growth. Leave the gossip for the others in the breakroom. Be cognizant of confidential information from other board members as well. When somebody says, "I'm telling you this in confidence," that means *do not share with others*. Lastly, exercise discretion when discussing personal challenges that may not directly impact your professional trajectory.

What if a board member wants to talk about personal topics? That's your call. At the end of the day, we are all regular people and have lives outside of work. You may see this nonwork type of conversation come up with your Accountability Partner or Buddy the most. It's helpful to discuss the in-play and out-of-play topics for each relationship during your onboarding and orientation process. Avoid sharing overly personal details or engaging in discussions that could blur the professional boundaries of your relationship.

Oversharing refers to the act of divulging more information than is necessary or appropriate in a given context. It can pertain to personal or professional matters and can occur in any type of relationship, including those between mentors and mentees. While open communication is important, oversharing can sometimes blur boundaries, create discomfort, or even harm the professional relationship.

Navigating Confidential and Sensitive Work-Related Matters

It's crucial to underscore the importance of exercising caution and discretion when engaging in conversations about confidential or sensitive matters pertaining to work. This includes refraining from discussing specific individuals or divulging confidential company information that could potentially harm professional relationships. It's significant to emphasize respecting boundaries and upholding confidentiality when discussing sensitive projects or initiatives.

Supporting the Stretch and Stress of Growth

How can you effectively support and nurture the growth of a Successor without burdening them with excessive stress or unattainable goals? One way is to refrain from highlighting their weaknesses or making comparisons with others. Instead, focus on offering constructive feedback, guidance, and support to assist them in their development and progress.

Action and Reflection

Chapter 9 is done! Here are a few things to noodle on before we dive into the ten seats on your personal board:

1. Have you developed the "pre-convo" agenda for your next professional development conversation?

2. What are your current in-play and out-of-play topics? Take a moment to evaluate how you have communicated the topics to stay away from with each board member and ask if there is anything else they'd like to add to the list. This can be revisited over time.

3. Are you asking too much of a specific board member? Taking up too much of their time? Go ahead and ask them about this in the next conversation.

4. Could you bring the start-stop-continue-shift methodology into other check-in and feedback conversations?

5. Would it make sense to formalize any of your professional relationships with an MDA?

Space for your notes and reflection.

CHAPTER 10

BUDDY:
THE PEER SUPPORT ADVISOR

"Alone we can do so little, together we can do so much."

*Helen Keller, a remarkable woman who overcame
deaf-blindness to become an accomplished author and
advocate for the disabled*

Among the boundless ocean of our professional journey, the waters can sometimes get choppy. Just as a life vest provides safety to a sailor amidst turbulent seas, a Buddy acts as your buoyant support in the professional realm. Close in experience, often navigating the same currents or facing the same winds, your Buddy offers tactical guidance, ensuring you don't drift off course. They might not have sailed the exact same route, but their proximity in professional waters offers invaluable peer-to-peer encouragement. Like the reassuring presence of a life vest, this relationship is characterized by its informal nature, providing a safe harbor for candid discussions and mutual growth. Your Buddy is there to ensure that, no matter how challenging the waters become, you're never navigating them alone.

I strongly suggest that your first Buddy be an internal employee (i.e., someone who works at the same company as you). Ideally, the Buddy seat on your PBA is always filled by an internal peer, someone within three years of your own work experience. You may find a Buddy in your onboarding cohort, at the coffee machine, at a work event, or through collaboration on a project. You may be assigned a Buddy in some corporate settings. It is not mandatory for your Buddy to have had the same job or career path as you. This relationship offers peer support, encouragement, and a safe space for discussions. This is the least formal relationship you will have on your personal board.

Two of the most prominent Buddies I had in my professional journey were Ben and Will. I met both serendipitously at work. We found ourselves at similar events and conferences, collaborated on teams, and over time, realized that we enjoyed working together. I mentioned Ben earlier, so let's talk about Will. He and I quickly developed a sense of trust and respect for one another and took time to learn about one another's lives inside and outside of work. I think we have now celebrated nearly a half dozen Fourth of Julys together! We discussed our career aspirations, daily work frustrations, and shared insights, perspectives, and sometimes very constructive feedback with each other. Over time, we found that our most productive conversations took place over guacamole and scotch. The bond we formed was powerful and remains strong to this day. Since we started as Buddies on our respective PBAs, we have worked on the same teams; he has worked for me, and I have worked for him. I look forward to what awaits us in the future!

Sometimes I refer to the Buddy board seat as a peer. Gallup talks about having a "best friend at work," and you may use your best friend as your Buddy—*if* they are up for being part of your professional development journey. We start with this role because you likely already have this person in your network today. Time to get a quick win and fill your first board seat!

Over the last few decades, "buddy programs" have become increasingly popular in corporate America. The goal of these programs is to connect new employees with a supportive and more experienced team member to help get them up and running sooner, establish a sense of belonging, make them feel comfortable, and guide them on some of the day-to-day happenings at work. You *do not* need to keep the assigned Buddy on your PBA if they are not a good fit.

Figure 35: The lifejacket represents the Buddy role on your PBA.

Goals for This Relationship

Be clear that the relationship is professional and when feedback is delivered, it is meant for growth and in the best interest of the receiver. Emphasize trust, confidentiality, and a willingness to offer unbiased support.

One of your initial goals together should be to complete the first iteration of your respective career maps, with multiple options at each phase. However, I suggest making the first pass on your own before delving into the Buddy review of the career map. An ongoing goal can be reducing your sense of isolation and increasing your feelings of belonging.

I used to work on a team with Marisa, and over time, she became a Buddy on my personal board, often helping as a mentor and Accountability Partner as well. However, I saw her primary role as Buddy. We both knew what was coming next when we walked into one another's office, shut the door, and cranked up Phil Collins. I grabbed the sticky notes and whiteboard markers, ready to listen!

Most of our Buddy conversations were related to career planning and "Should I stay or should I go (to my next job)?" Some of the topics we covered included:

1. Compensation and benefits
2. Job role and responsibilities
3. Company culture and environment
4. Location and commute
5. Long-term career path
6. The people!
7. Company stability and reputation
8. Work-life balance and stress levels
9. Additional perks and opportunities

In each conversation, while Phil serenaded us, we went through the following exercise: I drew up a table and asked her, "If you leave your current job now, what are the pros and cons? If you transition later, what are the pros and cons? If you never leave, what are the pros and cons?" We made sure to have at least three pros and cons for each of the three situations. It's OK to have more, but you should come up with at least three. We then put the table away and revisited it three to five days later. A few days after our second review, I suggested that she review the table with a Functional Mentor of hers and then with her Champion a few days after that. No, it's not a super-fast process, and we don't always have a lot of time to noodle on big-time career decisions, but I've found that unnecessary acceleration can lead to bigger issues. Try it out!

	Pros	Cons
If I Go Now		
If I Go Later		
If I Go Never		

Figure 36:The pros and cons table to populate when thinking through career transitions and new opportunities.

Contributions to Career Map

The Buddy role will be your informal feedback voice and peer perspective, helping you think through various paths and options you could take. I used to review my career map regularly with a few motivated coworkers during my first few years at Lockheed Martin. Sometimes we would meet one-on-one, and other times we would come together as a group—typically at a new restaurant or dive bar, on a hike, or during a volunteering activity. Ben taught me about "fishbowl feedback," and it was a great way to balance the cheerleader work with the butt-kicker support. We spent many nights in person and on phone calls, talking through our career maps and projecting if-thens while planning our professional futures. I am still very close with many of these board members, who are now dear friends.

Fishbowl feedback is a form of group discussion or facilitation method and can be useful for working through "hot topics" or collaborative ideation sessions. It is often used in meetings, workshops, and classrooms to ensure that everyone has an opportunity to speak and be heard. The technique gets its name from the idea of being "in the fishbowl," where a few participants are in the center of the group (akin to being in a fishbowl) while the rest of the group observes from the outside.

Here's how "fishbowl feedback" typically works:

- A small group (often three to six participants) sits in the center of the room, forming an inner circle. This is the "fishbowl."

- The rest of the participants form an outer circle around the fishbowl, observing the discussion.

- Choose one person "outside the bowl" to be the facilitator (this role can switch as the fishbowl swaps in and out).

- The inner circle discusses a specific topic while the outer circle listens without intervening.

- Members from the outer circle can join the discussion in the fishbowl, but for this to happen, someone from the inner circle usually has to leave, maintaining a consistent number of participants in the fishbowl.

- The process continues until the discussion reaches its conclusion or the facilitator ends it.

The fishbowl technique promotes active listening and ensures that a wide variety of voices are heard. By having a rotating group in the center, it prevents any single individual or group from dominating the conversation.

Conversation Flow

Buddy conversations will typically follow the "Board Conversation Flow" in Chapter 9. The details of this section outline some of the other topics you may address throughout the relationship.

Conversation 1

- Maintain a strong focus on getting to know the "real them."

Conversation 2

- Discuss career goals and outline (or refresh) both of your career maps.

- Talk about recent career challenges and growth opportunities, as well as navigating professional setbacks (big picture).

- Begin to discuss the in-play topics and the out-of-play topics.

Subsequent and Impromptu Conversations

- Plan out the next/future steps and weigh the pros and cons of each option.

- Talk through recent experiences at work and consider what could have gone better and perhaps what you could have done differently (stay focused on recent events).

- Discuss: What are each of you doing to continue your personal growth and continued learning?

You will likely call, direct message (on an internal messaging service), or text your buddy outside of these scheduled conversations. For example, you may see a new job opening, and you could hop on a quick call with your Buddy to talk through the pros and cons of it. You may have a rough day at work and need somebody to vent to. Buddies are also great to celebrate wins with, which can be especially helpful for people who hate "bragging" about themselves.

Frequency of Interaction

In the initial stages of this relationship, you might find yourself interacting with your Buddy on a daily or weekly basis. However, I recommend formal check-ins at least every two weeks through month six and may span to monthly by the end of the year. As your professional journey evolves, you might not collaborate as closely with your Buddy, but their role remains vital. Even when you ascend to executive roles, the value of a grounded peer or friend cannot be underestimated. While you can maintain your original Buddy throughout your professional growth, it's beneficial to reassess and potentially onboard new advisors every twelve months. This refresh aligns with the "rewire" phase of the "-iring" process in PBA development. For instance, as an executive, you might find it enriching to have a fellow executive as your Buddy.

Like all relationships on your PBA, you'll likely find the need for more frequent meetings initially, tapering off as you establish a rhythm. However, for the Buddy role, ensure that there's no more than a month-long gap between your discussions.

What to Avoid

Balance your work relationship and professional boundaries (the in-play and out-of-play topics). Keep the boundaries! Of course, this is easier said than done. A way to make this easier is to spend a little more time on the goals and expectations phase early in the relationship. Talk through in greater detail what is truly in and out of play. Talk through what to do when a topic begins to veer away from "in-bounds" conversation. It can be as simple as, "Hey, let's get back to our scheduled programming and the planned agenda; I think we are getting too far off topic."

Another pitfall is breaking confidentiality. You are close and will dive deep into some complicated topics. Be sure to not share these confidential conversations outside of this relationship.

Finally, do not ask too much of the buddy without giving value to them in return. Relatedly, do not take up too much of their time and abuse the "open lines" of communication—2 a.m. texts about a new project management training are not always appreciated. (Ben can tell you stories of how I abused that!)

When We Are a Buddy (Filling a Board Seat)

This role is reciprocal. Be sure you make clear the expectations and out-of-play items. Take time to listen and keep a balance of give and take.

Action and Reflection

As we wrap up Chapter 10 start to think about the person best to fit your Buddy board seat!

1. Who can you add as your Buddy to your PBA? If you have two to three in mind, who is your "first-round draft pick?" Could the others fill other board seats?

2. Are you a Buddy for somebody else? Would it make sense to reach out to a person who was a Buddy for you previously during an onboarding process or in another program? You may be surprised how much it means to them to just say hello and see what's going on in their life now.

3. Shout-out to the great work Dawn Klinghoffer is doing at Microsoft as the head of people analytics. Read more about corporate Buddy programs on the companion website or in her 2019 HBR article, Every New Employee Needs an Onboarding "Buddy."

Below is the first update to our PBA (comparison) matrix that was mentioned at the start of Part II. We will populate a table similar to this for the following nine chapters and board seats.

Buddy	
Seat Details	Peer Support Advisor
Icon Recap	Life Jacket—keeps you afloat and close in all waters (stormy and calm)
Experience	Within 1–3 Yrs of yours
Internal vs. External	Internal
My Goal with Them	Gain peer support and advice, how things work and operate, similar challenges, discussion related to work-life balance
Career Map Contributions	Develop first draft and brainstorm "if this, then that" over time
Their Background	Can be similar to yours or vary, important that you get along and they fill most of the "Yes" boxes on the Board Prospect Preparation Checklist from Chapter 3
Meeting Frequency	Daily at start, then weekly and every other week; may be monthly by end of the year

Figure 37: Summarizes the Buddy details of the PBA Matrix.

CHAPTER 11

ACCOUNTABILITY PARTNER:

THE COMMITMENT ENFORCER AND RESPONSIBILITY ADVISOR

"Accountability is the glue that ties commitment to results."

Bob Proctor, author of The Law of Attraction and the YouTube hit video "The Secret"

In the vast voyage of our professional lives, there are moments when the tides of stress rise and the horizon appears distant. Envision your Accountability Partner as the anchor that steadfastly keeps you grounded amidst these unpredictable waves. As challenges surge, they serve as the stabilizing force, consistently reminding you of your commitments and direction. Not the captain or the navigator, they are a fellow sailor, intimately familiar with the highs and lows of the journey. Just like the unwavering anchor that holds fast during stormy seas, your Accountability Partner ensures that amidst the frenetic pace of success, you find moments to pause, reflect, and recharge. They guarantee that no matter the intensity of the currents, you remain anchored to your goals and true direction.

Of course, other board members will hold you accountable, but it is unlikely that you will get the same commitment and stern stance from them. You are committing to your Accountability Partner, and they are committing to you. A study from the American Society of Training and Development (now the Association for Talent Development) found that committing to someone else significantly increases the likelihood of a person achieving their goal. According to the findings, people have a 65 percent chance of completing a goal if they commit to someone else. And if they have specific accountability appointments with a person they've committed to, they will increase their chance of success by up to 95 percent.[21]

In the early stages of your professional journey, it might be tempting to have your Buddy or Functional Mentor also serve as your Accountability Partner. However, as you advance, it becomes crucial to separate these roles; merging them risks diluting the unique value each brings and creates a single point of vulnerability. While a Buddy offers peer support and informal guidance, and a Mentor provides direction based on their experience and wisdom, an Accountability Partner's primary role is to keep you true to your commitments. By diversifying these roles, you harness the specialized support each offers, ensuring a more robust and balanced advisory board.

The Accountability Partner board seat likely has within ten years of your level of experience. They are a peer on a similar journey, understanding the challenges and joys of pursuing success. This relationship, akin to a workout companion for both your professional and personal life, is indispensable. They enforce your commitment to growth while reminding you of the importance of balance, ensuring you never feel isolated or overwhelmed.

Figure 38: The anchor represents the Accountability Partner role on your PBA.

21 Wissman, B. 2018. "An Accountability Partner Makes You Vastly More Likely to Succeed." *Entrepreneur.* https://www.entrepreneur.com/leadership/an-accountability-partner-makes-you-vastly-more-likely-to/310062.

Goals for This Relationship

Navigating the intricacies of the professional world requires guidance, support, and a touchstone to keep you grounded. An Accountability Partner provides this foundation. As you engage with this board member, here are the goals to aim for when getting started:

1. Use your Accountability Partner as a trusted confidante, someone to share your feelings, concerns, and dreams with. They are there to listen without judgment, helping you process your thoughts and emotions.

2. Leverage this board seat to help you stay on track with your personal and professional objectives. Share your goals and aspirations with them and encourage them to gently remind you if you seem to deviate.

3. Discuss your work-life balance with your Accountability Partner. They can help to remind you of the need to focus on personal well-being and mental health, ensuring you don't get lost in the grind or burn out.

4. Share your personal definition of success with this board member. They can help ensure you're not swayed by external pressures, keeping you aligned with your own standards and aspirations.

5. Rely on this person to act as a mirror to reflect upon your achievements. Together, celebrate your milestones and appreciate the nuances of your journey.

Engaging with your Accountability Partner should be characterized by open, genuine conversations. Focus on sharing and active listening. The relationship isn't about finding instant solutions but about validating experiences, reinforcing strengths, and ensuring continuous alignment with your goals.

While working on this section, I met with some of the US Surgeon General's staff, and they shared some startling statistics about mental health concerns at all age levels. This quote stood out the most.

"Our epidemic of loneliness and isolation has been an underappreciated public health crisis that has harmed individual and societal health. Our relationships are a source of healing and well-being hiding in plain sight—one that can help us live healthier, more fulfilled, and more productive lives. Given the significant health consequences of loneliness and isolation, we must prioritize building social connections the same way we have prioritized other critical public health issues such as tobacco, obesity, and substance use disorders. Together, we can build a country that's healthier, more resilient, less lonely, and more connected." [22]

US Surgeon General Dr. Vivek Murthy

Figure 39: A sign near Hermosa Beach, California. It belonged to one of my Accountability Partners, Steve; he told me that it was a gift from a friend. After some research, I think this work of art was developed by Second Hand Nature by Hand.

22 U.S. Department of Health and Human Services. 2023. "New Surgeon General Advisory Raises Alarm about the Devastating Impact of the Epidemic of Loneliness and Isolation in the United States." https://www.hhs.gov/about/news/2023/05/03/new-surgeon-general-advisory-raises-alarm-about-devastating-impact-epidemic-loneliness-isolation-united-states.html.

Contributions to Career Map

While an Accountability Partner isn't responsible for creating or altering your career map, they play an essential role in ensuring you're making progress along your chosen path. They can also provide useful feedback and perspectives that can shape your decision-making processes.

As valuable as your Accountability Partner is to helping you stay on top of what to get done, they can also be the voice of reason helping you stay out of the "no wake zone" and knowing when *not* to do something. It's been helpful for me to review the previous four weeks on my calendar with my Accountability Partner and assess what I could or should have done differently with my time. Mostly it's me talking through things, and the Accountability Partner is simply a facilitator. Then we go look at the upcoming four weeks and I realize how many things can get pushed back a month or a quarter or deleted entirely. "Less but better" can really help!

Conversation Flow

Accountability Partner conversations will typically follow the "Board Conversation Flow" in Chapter 9. The details of this section outline some of the other topics you may address throughout the relationship.

Conversation 1

- Talk about what motivates you most.
- Discuss how to react when I do not complete my goals.
- Brainstorm how to get me back on track.
- Ask how they hold themselves accountable and if they have an Accountability Partner.

Conversations After

- Share perspectives on best practices around work-life balance.
- Ask: What did you do last, what will you do next, and what will you do differently if needed?
- Determine how to take small steps and break down areas where you have faltered to get back on track. Think of some small wins to help bring back the confidence.
- Celebrate the wins along the way! Develop a "rewards for winning list" of things that you get to do or buy or not do when you hit certain goals or milestones on your career map and in life.
- Think about what people may say at your funeral if you were to pass away tomorrow. Is that how you want people to remember you? Are there some things to shake up and shift now? We do not have to wait for a bad moment to hit us to recalibrate. Sometimes it takes an outside perspective and somebody who really cares to get us back onto the right path or to realize we are on the totally wrong path and find a new one.

When I was first writing this chapter, I got a text from one of my first Accountability Partners, Steven, asking to chat for a few minutes. (I am realizing that I have had a lot of Steves and Stevens on my PBA over the years!) We have been co-Accountability Partners for a long time. I keep an ongoing note on my phone about our discussions and commitments, and I schedule a follow-up reminder each time we chat. In this particular instance, he wanted to bounce some ideas off of me while thinking through his next career jump.

You might wonder, "Why is he not a Buddy?" The focus of our relationship is more strategic. We have set goals that we share with one another, review our progress, and give feedback on wins and shortcomings. Additionally, we have both pivoted in our work a few times and worked together to redefine the goals for our next chunks of work as needed.

Frequency of Interaction

This is a role you want to fill on your PBA as soon as possible, and do your best never to let it go empty. The frequency of conversations will be greater at the start of the relationship, then it will reduce slightly. Start by meeting twice a month for the first two to three months, then extend the frequency to at least once every four to eight weeks over time.

What to Avoid

Your Accountability Partner is (likely) not a professional coach or therapist, so it's important not to treat them as such. While they can provide support and encouragement, they may not have the tools or resources to handle severe emotional or psychological distress. In such cases, it's essential to seek professional help.

They also aren't responsible for your progress. They can remind you of your goals and commitments, but the responsibility to take action remains with you.

Finally, avoid being overly dependent on your Accountability Partner. The goal is to enhance your self-accountability, not to become reliant on external validation or motivation. Your partner is there for support, but the journey is ultimately yours.

When We Are the Accountability Partner

When you step into the role of an Accountability Partner for another individual, it's essential to recognize that while the core tenets of the relationship mirror what you'd seek in a partner for yourself, there's a unique responsibility that comes with being on the guiding side. Firstly, genuine respect for the individual you'll be supporting is paramount. This foundation of mutual respect will drive the relationship forward, ensuring that guidance and feedback are provided constructively. It's also crucial to be in tune with their professional and personal aspirations. This alignment ensures that your support is directed and purposeful. Effective communication becomes your cornerstone; you should be adept at not just providing feedback, but also actively listening to their concerns and challenges. Committing to regular check-ins and being consistently available solidifies the relationship's intent and trajectory. The ability to empathize with their challenges while also offering encouragement and sometimes a gentle nudge is a balance that you, as their partner, will need to master. Finally, shared core values will ensure a smoother journey, minimizing misunderstandings and fostering a sense of camaraderie and mutual growth.

Action and Reflection

As we wrap up Chapter 11, start to think about what kinds of attributes you truly need in an Accountability Partner and how they can help you on your various journeys in life.

1. Do you have a professional peer that "checks in" on you personally (not just about "work things" all the time)?

2. Have you discussed with your Accountability Partner how to get back on track if you do not meet certain goals?

3. Is it time to revisit your ikigai, purpose, personal mission, and "why?" Sometimes this is a very helpful way to get back on track when we miss goals or milestones on our professional plans.

Accountability Partner

Seat Details	Commitment Enforcer and Responsibility Advisor
Icon Recap	Anchor—keeps you steady, holds you to your word while the swirls of life try to push you around on your journey
Experience	Within 10 Yrs of yours
Internal vs. External	Likely External for most of your professional journey; may add Internal Accountability Partner within your company midcareer
My Goal with Them	Accountability, motivation, mental health and emotional well-being, stress management, work-life harmony; focus on defining and refining goals over time and turning them into accomplishments in small steps
Career Map Contributions	Help you take small steps toward the immediate future; take time to step back and ensure that near-term future steps are in alignment with long-term aspirations
Their Background	Can vary, but conversation and feedback style should be in strong alignment with yours; helpful to be in similar functions (leadership vs. individual contributor), but industry can vary drastically
Meeting Frequency	Twice monthly first 2–3 months, then every 4–8 weeks over time

Figure 40: Summarizes the Accountability Partner details of the PBA Matrix.

Space for your notes and reflection.

CHAPTER 12:

FUNCTIONAL MENTOR:
THE EXPERIENCED GUIDE AND INSIDE ADVISOR

"A great mentor helps you see the potential within yourself that you didn't realize was there."

Catherine Pulsifer, speaker and author who focuses on personal development, success, and life challenges

Every professional embarking on a developmental journey needs a reliable guide to navigate the tides of career growth. The Functional Mentor, represented as the compass on your PBA, serves as this steadfast guide, directing you with clarity and wisdom. They are your touchstone in the world of professional development, with a reservoir of knowledge derived from years of experience.

While the Buddy offers camaraderie and the Accountability Partner ensures commitment to your objectives, the Functional Mentor stands as your beacon, illuminating your path with insights and foresight. This mentor ideally treads five to ten years ahead of you, providing wisdom that comes from having been in your position and understanding the nuances of your challenges and aspirations. Their interactions and perhaps even collaborations with or under your Supervisor grant them a unique perspective on your current role and its future trajectory.

This mentor's role is distinctly navigational and twofold: they guide you based on their triumphs, imparting strategies that have brought them success, and they also share lessons from their missteps, ensuring you're aware of potential pitfalls. This balanced guidance equips you with a holistic perspective, helping you discern not only what to do but also what to avoid.

Consider legendary mentor-mentee dynamics from cinema to further illuminate the essence of the Functional Mentor role. In *Star Wars*, Yoda, the venerable Jedi Master, takes on the role of Functional Mentor to Luke Skywalker, a young aspiring Jedi. Yoda's profound wisdom and teachings not only help Luke harness the power of the Force but also assist him in overcoming personal challenges and self-doubt. Yoda's guidance is pivotal in molding Luke into the Jedi he aspires to be, illustrating the transformative power of a mentor who has both the expertise and the patience to guide their mentee.

Similarly, in *The Karate Kid*, Mr. Miyagi serves as both a karate instructor and life coach to young Daniel LaRusso. Underneath the karate lessons lie deeper teachings about respect, discipline, and balance. Mr. Miyagi's unconventional training methods, from waxing cars to painting fences, impart more than just martial arts techniques; they provide Daniel with a foundation of values and principles that serve him well both in and out of the dojo. This relationship underscores the idea that a true mentor imparts wisdom that transcends the immediate skill or topic at hand, equipping the mentee with tools for holistic growth.

Drawing parallels to the professional world, these iconic mentor-mentee relationships emphasize the profound impact a dedicated mentor can have. Much like Yoda or Mr. Miyagi, a Functional Mentor in the professional realm does more than just provide guidance on job-specific tasks. They instill values, offer broader life wisdom, and foster both personal and professional growth, ensuring their mentees are equipped to navigate the multifaceted challenges of their careers.

Figure 41: The compass represents the Functional Mentor role on your PBA.

Goals for This Relationship

Engaging with a Functional Mentor is a transformative experience, one that demands clarity in objectives to maximize the potential of the relationship. This engagement becomes even more profound when each goal is specific, measurable, achievable, realistic, timely, and truly personalized.

A cornerstone of this mentorship is the creation and refinement of a long-term career vision, complemented by a strategic plan that acts as a roadmap for your professional trajectory. This plan should not only chart out career growth but also delve into the nuances of skill acquisition and professional network expansion. Navigating the intricate dynamics of organizational politics and relationships is another pivotal goal. With your mentor's seasoned insights, you can better understand and maneuver within the power structures of your workplace.

Furthermore, the mentorship should be geared toward enhancing your leadership prowess and sharpening your decision-making skills. Additionally, you might consider setting objectives around mastering industry-specific knowledge, understanding emerging trends, and identifying potential growth areas or niches relevant to your field. These goals, while ambitious, are made achievable with your mentor's guidance.

You can't just set goals and hope your mentor helps you achieve them, however; being a proactive mentee is essential. Embrace a mindset that is voracious for learning, continuously seeks guidance, and is committed to both personal and professional evolution. The onus falls on you to drive the relationship, from scheduling meetings to actively seeking feedback on your performance and growth areas. Engage in discussions not only about recent career events but also about how to anticipate and respond to future challenges. You might also explore topics like ethical decision-making, building resilience, and fostering innovation. Regular reflection on this mentorship journey, active listening, feedback implementation, and setting new goals ensures the relationship remains dynamic and continually aligned with the SMARTY methodology.

Frequency of Interaction

The frequency of mentoring conversations will be greater at the start of the relationship and will then slow slightly. I suggest starting by meeting two times per month for the first three months and then once monthly for the next nine months (which completes a full one-year cycle).

It's completely acceptable to engage your Functional Mentor in conversations beyond formally scheduled sessions. I distinctly remember an incident in Florida where I was overseeing a challenging situation with my team. Believing I was making the right choices, I pushed forward with a project direction. However, immediately after our meeting, I was bombarded with negative feedback. Comments like "I can't believe you did that" and stern messages from my colleagues filled my inbox. I had inadvertently overlooked a crucial group whose work would be affected by my decisions. Feeling like I was under scrutiny, I reached out to Daniel, who had once been my Supervisor and had transitioned into the Functional Mentor role, for guidance.

I sent him a direct message (DM), quickly followed by a text asking for urgent advice. Within the hour, we were discussing the situation privately over a call. After I described the issue, Daniel posed some clarifying questions. He then shared his method for initiating projects and asked how I might have approached things differently with hindsight. I lightheartedly responded that I wished our conversation had taken place forty-eight hours earlier. Daniel laughed, reminding me that as a mentor, he was there to guide me both proactively and reactively.

Contributions to Career Map

Functional Mentors serve as career compasses, guiding us through the often-turbulent seas of our professional journey. Their role is not to hand us a step-by-step manual but rather to shine a light on the myriad pathways tailored to our aspirations. They bring to the table a treasure trove of insights, experiences, and perspectives that can be transformative for our careers. Here are some ways a functional mentor can bolster our career mapping:

By evaluating your strengths and areas for improvement, they can help **pinpoint key skills you should develop** to align with your career goals.

They can **introduce you to influential figures** (supporting the Sponsor role) within and outside of your industry, thereby fostering connections that could lead to potential job opportunities or collaborations.

With their experience, they can provide insights into **navigating the intricate dynamics of an organization,** ensuring you position yourself advantageously.

They can serve as a sounding board, **offering constructive feedback** on your ideas, strategies, or plans and ensuring you're on a viable path. (This makes them more strategic than the Buddy.)

By challenging your thought processes, they **encourage you to think more strategically** about your career moves, ensuring long-term success.

They can **recommend courses, workshops, or seminars** that can further your knowledge and skills in your chosen field.

While it's great to dream big, a functional mentor **helps you ground your aspirations, ensuring** you set achievable and meaningful goals.

Sushi Strategy

One memorable evening, I found myself sharing sushi with Matt in Virginia. Introduced to me through a family connection, Matt, with his towering presence and mutual love for basketball, was an unlikely yet invaluable mentor at the beginning of my PBA journey. At this nascent stage, I was just dipping my toes into the world of professional mentorship. Looking back, I wish I had had this book to better understand the goldmine of guidance Matt was offering!

Matt seamlessly played multiple roles for me: an external Functional Mentor, a Champion, and at times a Sponsor. During our meal, he posed an insightful question about my inclination toward individual contribution or management. Though undecided, I was leaning toward management. Matt highlighted the significance of gaining profit and loss (P&L) experience, a concept that was then unfamiliar to me. He urged me to delve into it, engage with seasoned professionals, undertake a cost account manager (CAM) training, and explore a stretch assignment in a P&L-centric role.

Fast-forward five years: Kim, my then-Supervisor, and Rich, who later transitioned into my Functional Mentor (and was also my P90X workout companion), played crucial roles in my realizing Matt's advice. Under Rich's guidance, I underwent the CAM training, took on a minor P&L stretch assignment, and subsequently secured an internal program manager position to further hone this skill. These experiences were pivotal when I later joined a smaller organization where P&L mastery was essential.

A quick final note: Kim's instrumental role in my journey will be covered in greater detail in Chapter 19, which focuses on the Supervisor's role in the PBA. While Kim was pivotal in setting the stage, it was Rich who seamlessly transitioned into the Functional Mentor role, guiding me through the intricacies of P&L, an area of expertise my former Functional Mentor, Matt, had emphasized years earlier.

Conversation Flow

Functional Mentor conversations will typically follow the "Board Conversation Flow" in Chapter 9. The details of this section outline some of the other topics you may address throughout the relationship.

Conversation 1

- Delve into your Mentor's experiences. They'll likely be curious about your journey too.

- Present your career map to provide a clear picture of your aspirations and ground the mentorship with tangible goals.

- Ask if they've mentored others. If they have, understanding what worked and what didn't in those relationships can set the tone for a more productive partnership.

- Understand their preferred method of imparting advice and guidance so there are no misunderstandings in the future.

Conversation 2

- What are the pivotal milestones I should be targeting in my career?

- Can you recall challenges you encountered at my career stage? How did you navigate them?

- What growth opportunities and stretch assignments should be on my radar?

- How might I best leverage my strengths for optimal career advancement?

- Are there foreseeable roadblocks, and how would you recommend I address them?

Conversation 3

- What actions or approaches should I start implementing?

- What habits or mindsets do I need to stop?

- What am I doing well that I should continue?

- What requires a slight adjustment or shift in approach?

- Ask questions about emerging trends, positioning for promotions, and strategies for balancing professional growth with personal well-being can offer a holistic view of your career landscape.

Conversation 4

- Explore opportunities beyond the immediate mentor-mentee dynamic. Ask them for warm referrals or introductions to other professionals who can provide complementary insights or opportunities.

- Discuss any open seats on one another's boards, suggesting potential roles or individuals who could further enrich your professional journeys.

What to Avoid

Be sure not to ask too much of your mentor and overstep the boundaries of the support and guidance they are providing to you. An easy way to know if you are at risk of this is to ask them outright: "Am I asking too much of you?" During one of your goal-review conversations, you could also ask, "Are our conversations in alignment with the foundational expectations that we set early on?"

Do not let your mentor create a "Mini-Me" and tell you how to do things exactly the way they did them.

When We Are a Mentor to Others

As you progress professionally, opportunities will arise for you to guide others through their career mazes. Embracing Stephen Covey's principle to "seek first to understand, then to be understood" is paramount. Before jumping to conclusions or offering solutions, deeply understand your mentee's challenges and aspirations. Adopt a coaching mentality, but remember that there's a difference between coaching and mentoring. A coach often instructs, while a mentor guides. It's crucial to lead your mentee to conclusions rather than dictating steps; this enables them to own their decisions and learn organically. Although it might be tempting, given your experience, to solve every problem they present, refrain. Instead, share your experiences, letting them navigate the solution-finding process. Encourage a mindset of continuous learning and keep them updated with the latest industry trends. Constructive feedback, delivered empathetically, can also be a cornerstone of their growth, along with introductions to diverse contacts in your network. Periodically reflect on the direction your mentorship is taking to ensure it remains productive for both parties. Ultimately, effective functional mentorship isn't about providing all the answers but rather enabling the mentee to discover them, enriching both of your professional journeys.

Action and Reflection

How can you start to take advantage of "Yoda quality" mentoring wisdom now that we have concluded Chapter 12?

1. Do you have a Functional Mentor on your PBA who is not also doubling to fill another board seat?

2. Do you ask your Functional Mentor for advice and guidance that aligns with your future career map plans?

3. When did you last ask a mentor about the hardships and setbacks they faced?

4. Would it be valuable to ask your mentor(s) about the education and certifications they explored while at your career stage and if they would have done things differently if they could go back and do it again?

Functional Mentor	
Seat Details	Experienced Guide and Inside Advisor
Icon Recap	Compass—guide you on your path, but not directly moving you or steering your journey in the day-to-day work
Experience	Within 5–10 Yrs of yours
Internal vs. External	Likely Internal for first and second Functional Mentor; may add External Functional Mentor over time
My Goal with Them	Gain insights from their experience, career advice, leadership development; tips on industry trends
Career Map Contributions	Early to midcareer—help shape and refine your career map based on their own experience
Their Background	Similar background and career journey as you, ideally have been in your position before, maybe even worked with your Supervisor before
Meeting Frequency	Every other week for first 3 months, then monthly; may extend to 6–8 weeks by end of the year

Figure 42: Summarizes the Functional Mentor details of the PBA Matrix.

CHAPTER 13:

CROSS-FUNCTIONAL MENTOR:

THE SPECIALIST MENTOR AND OUTSIDE ADVISOR

"The delicate balance of mentoring someone is not creating them in your own image but giving them the opportunity to create themselves."

Steven Spielberg, a pretty solid moviemaker

In our voyage across the vast oceans of professional life, sometimes the direct route isn't the only path to treasure. Just as a key unlocks hidden chambers and reveals unexpected treasures, the Cross-Functional Mentor introduces you to uncharted territories of expertise, offering insights that might not be immediately visible on your direct course.

This mentor differs from your Functional Mentor in that they have had different roles and experiences than you. If you sail the engineering seas, they might have charted the waters of legal bays or navigated the currents of marketing channels. With a wealth of knowledge amassed over years, often a decade or more, they offer perspectives from different horizons. It's OK for this mentor to come from outside your organization if you cannot find one internally (but give it a solid try first, please); however, like your Functional Mentor, they will still have approximately five to ten more years of experience than you.

While it's invaluable to have a guide from your own fleet, sometimes the most profound insights come from those who've sailed different seas. Your Cross-Functional Mentor is that special key, opening doors to diverse realms and ensuring you gain a holistic view of the vast professional world.

I realized the need for a Cross-Functional Mentor when I was a first-time program manager, consistently working with engineers and senior program managers (PMs). I noticed a mover and shaker in my organization, but she was neither a PM nor an engineer. Michelle was in communications and marketing, and everybody loved her. Serendipitously, I decided to ask her more about her experiences and how she had progressed professionally. She shared interesting perspectives about the organization and how her work impacted our external image and helped our internal group flourish . . . all because she actually knew what was going on. Communication is incredibly impactful, and it's not an easy feat, especially given that we worked with a hybrid team distributed across half the states in the continental United States. Over time, I realized that it was useful to go to Michelle for advice on certain work topics to which she brought a totally neutral and fresh perspective. She became my Cross-Functional Mentor, and our relationship not only benefitted me but even helped break down some of the silos and schisms between our functions.

Figure 43: The key represents the Cross Functional Mentor role on your PBA.

Goals for This Relationship

Engaging with a Cross-Functional Mentor isn't meant to produce a carbon copy of your Functional Mentor's advice; it's about acquiring a kaleidoscope of insights. By understanding how different functions in an organization impact and are impacted by your role, you develop a more well-rounded approach to your career. Your goals could include:

- Gaining insights from a different functional perspective
- Enhancing your understanding of the broader organizational ecosystem
- Learning how different departments and functions interplay and affect each other (plus any "bad blood" from the past)
- Leveraging their unique experience to identify potential collaboration points or synergies that can benefit both of your roles and/or projects

Frequency of Interaction

The frequency of mentoring conversations will be greatest at the start of the relationship and then slow slightly. I suggest meeting twice each month for the first two months and then once every six to eight weeks for the next ten months (completing a full one-year cycle).

Contributions to Career Map

The contributions of your Cross-Functional Mentor will be similar to those of your Functional Mentor, albeit helping you think about things in a different manner. They can guide you on the near-term "future" items on your career map and also provide guidance and insight from their experiences on the steps others took—what worked and what didn't. They may even play dumb sometimes, asking you "Then what?" or "What else?" or "And if that doesn't work at first, then what?" questions as you keep progressing.

Owen was a Cross-Functional Mentor to me for several years. Interestingly, our camaraderie began on the basketball courts of DC However, our routine meetings typically found us in his spacious corner office in Washington, DC, with him sipping tea while I drank coffee. Owen's realm of expertise is in real estate, whereas I've navigated the fields of defense, engineering, tech, and human resources. Although our industries differ, Owen's leadership prowess and unparalleled networking skills consistently offered me invaluable insights. During a particularly crucial juncture in my career, Owen's guidance was indispensable. He was also instrumental in introducing

me to essential contacts and imparted strategies that continue to resonate deeply with my work. I once asked him about his tactics for managing diverse teams and for handling the ever-present unpredictable variables. He underscored the significance of hands-on leadership and strongly advocated for fostering a robust relationship with the customer. "Being authentic has immense value," he would remind me. Every time we'd conclude our discussions, I'd leave with pages brimming with actionable insights.

Some of the most helpful Cross-Functional Mentors in my life have helped me on my career planning journey. We put together a table of pros and cons (similar to the one shared in Chapter 11 on the Buddy). I also found the following career transition question quite helpful:

"Are you running away from something or are you running toward something?"

In answering this question I was able to reflect on a deeper level and better understand if I was indeed just trying to get out of a current situation or if I was actually super excited about the new gig and "running toward" it with excitement.

> ## "A mentor is someone who allows you to see the hope inside yourself."
>
> *Oprah Winfrey, a talk show host who mentored people on her show for 25 years and gave out a few "free cars" along the way*

Conversation Flow

Cross-Functional Mentor conversations will typically follow the "Board Conversation Flow" in Chapter 9. The details of this section outline additional topics you may address throughout the relationship.

Conversation 1

- Follow the same flow as the Functional Mentor in Chapter 12.

Conversation 2

- Dive deeper into the specifics of your mentor's function.
- Ask about emerging trends in their domain.
- Seek to understand how their department or function interacts with or impacts others, like yours.

Ongoing Conversations

- Discuss the mutual benefits of this relationship. Are there areas where you can offer them insights or assistance?

- Consider discussing the broader organizational culture, politics, and dynamics from their perspective.

Joe is another Cross-Functional Mentor with a very technical background; he could probably fly a plane with the power of Excel (no joke). He has been like a professional father figure to me and joined me on my mission to build my tech startup after being one of our first users of the software in late 2018. Joe always reminds me that "free advice is worth every penny you pay for it." When I asked Joe for advice on solving technical problems, he reflected on a few of his past experiences and somehow always came up with a good, bad, and "middle" scenario. He never told me exactly what to do, but he always guided me in the right direction and suggested some "if you do this, then that may happen" situations. He provided a valuable alternate perspective from the nongovernment manufacturing and pharmaceutical industries. Joe also ended each conversation with an uplifting motivational message to fuel me for the rest of the day—which I loved!

What to Avoid

As with the Functional Mentor, ensure the relationship remains mutually beneficial. While it's essential to seek their input, also be open to offering your insights where relevant. Always respect their time and expertise and ensure you're not overburdening them with frequent or lengthy requests.

When We Are a Cross-Functional Mentor to Others

Taking on the role of a Cross-Functional Mentor offers you a chance to view your expertise through fresh eyes. While guiding, remember the words of Alexandra K. Trenfor: "The best teachers are those who show you where to look but don't tell you what to see." Offer direction, introduce them to your world, but let them draw their conclusions.

Action and Reflection

As we wrap up Chapter 13, start to think about what you can be doing today and what you are maybe already doing but just not tracking ... yet!

1. Reflect on your current professional network. Who can serve as a Cross-Functional Mentor for you?

2. Are there certain functions that you know little about in your organization? Might be a good place to fill the gap with a Cross-Functional Mentor!

3. Do you feel tension with other teams or functions at work? The Cross-Functional Mentor may be able to help bridge some of the divides and mend the working relationships!

Cross-Functional Mentor	
Seat Details	Specialist Mentor and Outside Advisor
Icon Recap	Key—open insights to other opportunities and experiences you may not be part of or aware of
Experience	Within 5–10 Yrs of yours
Internal vs. External	Internal (can be external if you really cannot find one internally)
My Goal with Them	Gain knowledge about functions outside of your current role and past experience; exposure to other transferable skills
Career Map Contributions	Map out trajectory aligned with your ambitions, interests, strengths; multiple backup options or pivot opportunities at each future stage
Their Background	Different work experience from yours (if you're engineering, they may be marketing, legal, sales, or other non engineering roles)
Meeting Frequency	Twice monthly first 2 months, then every 6–8 weeks through end of the year

Figure 44: Summarizes the Cross-Functional Mentor details of the PBA Matrix.

Space for your notes and reflection.

CHAPTER 14:

COACH:

THE PROJECT-BASED
TACTICAL ADVISOR

*"The greatest good you can do for another is not just to
share your riches, but to reveal to them their own."*

Benjamin Disraeli, British statesman, and novelist
from the 1800s who twice served as Prime Minister
of the United Kingdom

In the symphony of our professional journey, there are times when we need a specific
tune and a focused rhythm to guide us through uncharted waters. The Coach, symbolized
by the whistle, serves as this rhythm setter.

Just as the whistle calls attention, sets a pace, and signals shifts during a game, a Coach
narrows your focus. You may have had a coach in sports, a teacher when learning to
play an instrument, or even a tutor to study for an important standardized test or
exam. A Coach's engagement, often bound by the confines of a specific project or
timeline, is a concentrated burst of guidance, much like the sharp call of a whistle
amidst the ambient noises.

I distinctly remember hiring my first professional Coach, Dan, at a pivotal juncture in my entrepreneurial journey. As my business was expanding, a pressing need for increased sales emerged. While I had mentors offering general guidance, there was a palpable void: I yearned for deliberate, tactical advice delivered consistently. Dan, a renowned sales coach, had been on my radar for some time. Many of my mentors lauded his expertise, but my initial mindset was one of skepticism: *Why would I need a Coach? I can navigate this on my own.* But reality painted a different picture; despite my efforts, sales stagnated, and growth was elusive.

Taking the plunge, I enlisted Dan's services—and I've never looked back. If given a chance to revisit that decision, I'd hire him again in a heartbeat, only wishing I'd done it sooner. Dan seamlessly transitioned between various roles: a Coach providing structured guidance, a mentor sharing invaluable insights, and eventually a cherished friend, much like others in my PBA. He held me to account like a true Accountability Partner, facilitated strategic introductions akin to a Sponsor, and navigated me through challenges in a manner akin to a trusted Buddy or mentor. With his acute understanding of my journey and challenges, Dan guided me through taking incremental steps that cumulatively led to significant success. Under his guidance, our sales skyrocketed, and we witnessed a tenfold increase within a year.

But how does a Coach differ from a mentor? Great question! There are similarities and overlaps between the roles, but in the professional world, Coaches are the catalysts for growth. Think of a Coach as a tactical advisor who helps facilitate self-discovery and focused growth in specific areas. (Also, you pay them.) A mentor, on the other hand, shares wisdom and experiences to help strategically guide you rather than tell you exactly how to do things. (I have never heard of a mentor getting paid.) Coaches will bring specific frameworks to your situation, and they usually have a plan defined for you at the start of your relationship, while a mentor is on the path with you, mapping things out in real time and growing together.

Figure 45: The whistle represents the Coach role on your PBA.

Goals for This Relationship

In the realm of professional development, a Coach stands as a beacon of guidance and expertise. Often possessing a decade or more of experience than you, a Coach's insights become increasingly crucial as you navigate the middle stages of your career. Early in your professional journey, you might grapple with identifying areas where you need coaching. However, as you advance, not only will the frequency of your interactions with your Coach likely increase, but you might also find the need to collaborate with multiple Coaches, each bringing their distinct expertise to your table.

It's pivotal to understand that while Coaches bring invaluable experience, they typically come at a cost. However, as you ascend in your career and enjoy financial growth, this investment becomes more feasible and justified. After all, you're investing in unlocking your potential and ensuring long-term success. When working with a coach, especially in the early days, it is paramount to:

- **Be Specific:** Your goal should be laser-focused on the area you aim to improve or develop. Whether you're looking to master a new skill, pass a critical exam, achieve a fitness milestone, or prep for a pivotal event, clarity is paramount.

- **Define Success:** What does success in relation to your goal look like to you? Is it mastering a presentation technique, closing a significant deal, or leading a team project efficiently?

- **Choose Meaningful Metrics:** Once you've defined what success looks like, consider how you will evaluate or "test out" this newly honed skill. For instance, if your goal is public speaking, perhaps delivering a successful keynote address at a major event could be your benchmark for success.

Soon after I began realizing the benefits of hiring Dan as a sales Coach, I heeded the advice of another mentor to bring Cory onto my PBA as my LinkedIn Coach. We worked through challenges that I was facing in business and he helped me develop skills and habits to put strategy and plans into (successful) action. He did so in a way that resonated with me—after he tried to talk me out of hiring him to be my Coach. He made me think long and hard about whether or not this was truly the right "next move" on my career map. Again, the warm referrals from my PBA paid off, and I grew to become a LinkedIn influencer, which helped me recruit more business through the LinkedIn platform. Cory and I have gone on to work on multiple initiatives together, and he, too, has become a friend beyond my PBA.

Frequency of Interaction

Ask your Coach what works best in their experience when helping clients accomplish similar goals. They are the experts here. It is common to have numerous initial meetings at a condensed frequency and then move to a monthly or even bimonthly cadence.

Contributions to Career Map

Coaches are going to help add items to the third column on the career map—accomplishments, milestones, and achievements. They will work with you to develop these new skills.

The best coaches also challenge us, helping us ask ourselves if the work we're doing with them is actually necessary for what we want to achieve and where we want to go. They prompt us to consider, "Does this upcoming endeavor align with my purpose?" I have been on calls with Coach prospects, and they've talked me out of doing business with them. In one instance, I called the person back two years later and asked if I could still pay him to be my Coach. He is on my PBA as I write this section today!

The interplay between sports and professional development is profound. While our discussions have primarily centered around the professional realm, it's worth noting how sports and the lessons learned on the playing field can profoundly impact one's professional journey. Sports have been a cornerstone in my life, providing me with invaluable experiences that have influenced my professional trajectory. Consider any sports coaches you've encountered over the years. Can you recall the life lessons they shared? When was the last time you expressed gratitude for their guidance?

Two coaches in particular left an indelible mark on my journey: Coach Win Palmer and Coach Harry Leyland. These weren't just basketball coaches; they were life mentors who imparted lessons that extended far beyond the court's boundaries. They instilled in me principles that have proven invaluable in the business world. As I pen this section, I've recently learned of Coach Palmer's passing, and it's essential to dedicate this chapter to him, to Coach Leyland, and to all the other remarkable coaches who challenged me, broadened my horizons, and guided me toward realizing my true potential.

Conversation Flow

Conversations with your Coach will typically follow the "Board Conversation Flow" in Chapter 9. The details of this section outline some of the other topics you may address throughout the relationship.

Conversation 1

- Agree on your goals and expectations.
- Clearly define what "success" looks like and how you will measure it over time.

Conversation 2

- Share stories of the progress toward your goals and what you have tried since the previous conversation.
- Ask about situations they or their clients faced that could be relatable or similar.
- Ask clarifying questions.

Ongoing Conversations

- See how your Coach might help you put your new skill into action at an event, with another person, or in another capacity.
- Ask about referrals to see who else in their network you could or should have a conversation with (perhaps current or former clients).

What to Avoid

Do not ask your Coach to solve your problems for you. You brought them into your life for a reason, and now you have to do the work! Relatedly, do not overlook any homework they assign, and be sure to complete any to-do items before and after each session. You're paying them to help you, so get as much out of the sessions as you can!

When We Are a Coach to Others

In a coaching role, our emphasis should be on providing active guidance and fostering action-oriented progress. Unlike when playing the role of a mentor, as a coach, we offer specific direction on what steps to take. While still listening attentively and asking clarifying questions, our primary goal is to facilitate concrete action and measurable results. Our guidance should be practical and designed to help the individual achieve their goals and overcome challenges effectively. By taking an active role in steering them toward actionable steps, we can empower them to make substantial strides in their personal and professional development.

Action and Reflection

As the coaching chapter concludes, reflect on the following:

1. How have sports or other extracurricular activities influenced your professional mindset and work ethic?

2. Can you recall a mentor or Coach from your past who has significantly impacted your life journey? What was the most valuable lesson you learned from them?

3. How do you integrate the lessons learned from sports or other activities into your daily professional life?

4. Think about a skill or area in your professional life that has room for improvement. How might a Coach guide you in refining it?

5. Have you ever invested in your professional development? (The investment could be time, effort, money, or a combination of the three.) Reflect on the outcomes and whether they justified the investment.

6. As you progress in your career, are there specific milestones or challenges you foresee? How could a Coach help you navigate these?

Coach	
Seat Details	Project-Based Tactical Advisor
Icon Recap	Whistle—call for your attention when needed most and help you focus in near-term on what needs to be worked on
Experience	Usually at least 10+ Yrs
Internal vs. External	Usually External (may find internally in larger organizations)
My Goal with Them	Gain targeted guidance, develop expertise, enhance focused skill development
Career Map Contributions	Help achieve near-term accomplishments; may also help with certification milestones
Their Background	Expertise in their field, strong interpersonal skills and communication; background can be different, but must be adept at tailoring coaching to your needs and goals
Meeting Frequency	Follow guidance; may condense initial frequency, then move to monthly/every other month

Figure 46: Summarizes the Coach details of the PBA Matrix.

CHAPTER 15

SPONSOR:

THE INFLUENTIAL ADVOCATE AND SUPERCONNECTOR ADVISOR

"Success is achieved when we properly combine the who we know with the what we know."

Pete Schramm

In our professional odyssey, mentors act as compasses, fine-tuning our course and steering us through challenges. But it's the Sponsors who stand as the sturdy bridges, connecting us to new territories and untapped opportunities. Their role is emblematic of a bridge, creating pathways over obstacles, enabling smooth transitions, and helping us cross the gaps in our professional journeys. Fittingly, my initial encounters with Sponsors were rooted in Pittsburgh, a bridge-filled city that naturally symbolized the essence of sponsorship.

While both mentorship and sponsorship are integral to professional ascent, they serve distinct roles and cultivate varied dynamics in the relationship.

Here's a comprehensive breakdown:

Criteria	Mentor	Sponsor
Primary Role	Offer guidance, feedback; advice for professional growth	Advocate, leverage influence, provide critical connections and opportunities
Nature of Relationship	Regular one-on-one meetings focused on questions, advice skill-building	Less frequent interaction, emphasis on promoting brand, skills, achievements
Advocacy	Guide within boundaries of conversations	Bridge-building by introduction and endorsement
Visibility	Typically private; focused on personal and professional development	Visible within and beyond organizations, focused on making strategic introductions
Experience	Usually 5–10 years ahead	10+ years ahead in most instances
Risk	Committing their time and energy	Linking their reputation to your success; advocating on your behalf

Figure 47: Compares some of the high level criteria of a Mentor and a Sponsor.

Sponsors aren't just connectors; they're Superconnectors. Their advocacy doesn't represent a mere handout but a "hand up" as a vital bridge leading us to golden opportunities. Drawing from their expansive networks, they connect us with people and opportunities that can catalyze career growth. Their belief in our potential is so profound that they're willing to stake their reputation, and often also their time, to help us identify and reach new waypoints on our professional voyage.

Figure 48: The bridge represents the Sponsor role on your PBA.

Goals for This Relationship

Our primary goal is to grow with our Sponsor and allow their advocacy to be a springboard propelling us forward faster. We want to ensure we build strong rapport early on and make it easy for them to represent us and bring us into other conversations. This is another instance of clear communication being vital for success! Here is a short list of goals to achieve with your Sponsor:

- Navigate career trajectory with their influential advocacy.
- Learn to maneuver through organizational nuances and politics.
- Understand the intricacies of innovative career advancement (what worked for them).
- Elevate our professional persona, ensuring we are spoken about positively even when we are not "in the room where it happens."

Frequency of Interaction

Ask your Sponsor what works best with their schedule. I suggest meeting with your sponsor at least quarterly (once every three months) and keeping up this cadence throughout your entire career. Even if your Sponsor retires, see if they would be willing to hold an emeritus board seat.

An "emeritus" board seat is an honorary position given to a retired board member in recognition of their significant contributions and service to the organization. Typically, emeritus board members do not have voting rights, but may still participate in board discussions and offer their expertise.

Contributions to Career Map

A sponsor will focus mainly on the roles you envision for your future and help you map out the "if you do this, then you may be able to do that next." It's also helpful to discuss the transferable skills you might need in the future to determine small things you can incorporate into your work as your development continues. Our Sponsors can be our "people periscopes," helping us understand with whom else we should connect to share career map progress and ideas. I personally like to think of people I aspire to emulate and actually add their names to various future sections of my career map. The Sponsor will typically ask a few clarifying questions about these names and then help find ways to make introductions for informational discovery calls with those individuals. I then replace the name on my career map with my learnings from the conversation!

Conversation Flow

Sponsor conversations will typically follow the "Board Conversation Flow" in Chapter 9. The details of this section outline some of the other topics you may address throughout the relationship.

Conversation 1

- Let them know more about what fires you up and what you truly want to accomplish. When you make it easy for the Sponsor to know about your true passion, they can more easily know when and where to bring you up in discussions!

- Ask how they helped others gain visibility over time. What worked and what made things difficult?

Conversation 2

- Dive deeper into stretch assignments/opportunities or projects you could be involved in to increase your own visibility. (Start thinking about two or three of them now, so you can track them on the companion website.)

- Review your career map and your current PBA with your Sponsor so they see the full picture of your plan and current support structure. They may have suggestions on both the map and the board!
- Ask who you can learn from in their network to expand your own professional connections based on specific "future" items on your career map.

A "stretch assignment" worksheet is available on the companion website to help you work through what may make sense. Your sponsor will greatly appreciate your doing this as pre-work coming to the meeting with them.

Questions for Future Conversations

- What strategies can I implement to strengthen my personal brand and reputation?
- Are there any specific achievements or milestones I should focus on to enhance my professional profile?
- What strategies can I employ to foster mentorship and sponsorship relationships with others?

What to Avoid

Embarking on a relationship with a Sponsor can be transformative for your professional trajectory. However, it's pivotal to maintain a balance of respect, understanding, and mutual benefit. Here are potential pitfalls to avoid:

Overstepping Boundaries: A Sponsor's role is significant, as they can unveil hidden pathways in your professional journey. Treat their time as precious. Respect their boundaries by clarifying communication preferences and ensuring shared expectations.

Misjudging Communication Methods: A critical error I made was presumptuously using text messages for personal communication without first seeking my Sponsor's consent. It's a prime example of overlooking the personal touch and assuming comfort levels.

Being Overly Self-Centered: While it's natural to seek guidance, remember that true relationships are reciprocal. Don't let your interactions revolve solely around your needs. Engage, listen, and offer support in return.

Losing the Personal Element: Authentic connections aren't built on professional exchanges alone. Engage in heart-to-heart conversations, share personal stories, and express genuine interest in their life experiences.

> *"Strength does not come from winning.*
> *Your struggles develop your strengths."*
>
> *Arnold Schwarzenegger*

A personal lesson I learned the hard way underscores the importance of these guidelines. I had the privilege of being mentored by someone I'll refer to as Tim. Through Tim, I was introduced to Bob and subsequently to Beth. Having walked the path I was embarking on, these individuals were absolute goldmines of knowledge!

Initially, our relationships were dynamic and productive. I was learning and growing, but gradually I became too self-focused. I consistently sought advice and opportunities without reciprocating or showing genuine interest in their lives. I began texting them without inquiring about their preferred communication method, a clear breach of personal space. As time went on, my interactions became lopsided, focusing predominantly on my aspirations. This disregard for balance and the personal touch eroded the trust and rapport we had built.

As I ventured into entrepreneurship, I realized that I had lost these invaluable connections, primarily due to my insensitivity and lack of self-awareness. This experience was humbling. Now I emphasize active listening, mutual respect, and balanced interactions. I learned this lesson the hard way, and I encourage you to avoid my mistakes. (And if you ever witness me faltering, please hold me to account!)

When We Are a Sponsor to Others

When we are the Sponsor, a key priority is building a foundation of trust and respect. Take the time to understand their professional background, values, and career goals. As you put your brand on the line and make introductions on their behalf, remember that your advocacy can significantly impact their journey. To ensure a successful partnership in professional development, set clear boundaries and define expectations from the very beginning. Encourage them to approach this relationship with seriousness and maintain open and honest communication to address any challenges or adjustments that may arise.

Action and Reflection

We are more than halfway through the PBA, and the Sponsor may be the one that helps put more wind in your sails than you could have imagined. Think about how you can amplify your trust in this relationship through some of the following actions.

1. How do you clearly convey your aspirations, making it straightforward for others to connect you with new opportunities?

2. Reflect on the bridges you've crossed in your professional journey so far. How have Sponsors played a role?

3. In what ways can you reciprocate the advocacy and support provided by your Sponsors?

4. Do you have a list of transferable skills that you have been building or want to build?

5. What does an ideal (and not too stressful) stretch assignment look like for you?

6. When did you last review your full career map with a Sponsor and ask them for their feedback and suggestions?

Sponsor	
Seat Details	Influential Advocate and Superconnector Advisor
Icon Recap	Bridge—connect to new opportunities and people to cross gaps and stormy waters
Experience	10+ Yrs more and 1 (one) Level above you
Internal vs. External	Internal if at all possible
My Goal with Them	Amplify your brand and image while not in the room; networking opportunities and introductions
Career Map Contributions	Explore opportunities in an informational interview (see what may/may not be a good fit)
Their Background	Can vary or be similar; important they have been successful in their professional career
Meeting Frequency	Quarterly (at minimum every three months); keep cadence throughout career, even if they retire

Figure 49: Summarizes the Sponsor details of the PBA Matrix.

CHAPTER 16

CHAMPION:

THE STRATEGIC GUIDE AND "SPLIT-LEVEL" ADVISOR

"A true champion encourages others to be champions themselves."

Bernard Brogan, a heavily decorated Irish Gaelic footballer from the mid-2000s

In any professional journey, Champions emerge as lighthouses. They shine bright, illuminating our path and offering perspective, direction, and clarity amidst the vast ocean of career challenges and opportunities.

Champions are more than just career guides; they are strategic custodians, imbued with a wealth of wisdom and insights. Often positioned at least two levels above us in the organizational structure, Champions provide a panoramic view that is enriched by their vast experiences. This strategic positioning is optimal when they are within our current organization, as it maximizes the benefits of their guidance.

While mentors and Sponsors play significant tactical roles, Champions operate on a broader, more strategic canvas. They may not be daily fixtures in our immediate circles, but their belief in our potential and their strategic counsel can profoundly influence our professional direction. Envision them as board chairpersons in charge of strategic direction and aligning our overarching vision and aspirations.

You may also refer to the Champion board seat as a "split-level" relationship. A split-level meeting or relationship at work usually refers to interactions that involve individuals from different hierarchical levels within an organization. These can include meetings where senior leadership interacts directly with mid-level managers, front-line employees, or other staff members who are not typically in the same meetings. Our Sponsor may also be a "split level" but their function is more on advocating and connecting rather than strategic guidance and support focused on our development. The Champion can make introductions for us and connect us to others, but their primary focus is on connecting us to information, insights, and a broader awareness of how we fit into the larger organizational equation at work.

Figure 50: The lighthouse represents the Champion role on your PBA.

Goals for This Relationship

Champions help us stay grounded, reminding us that it's OK not to have all the details for the immediate next step on our career map figured out. There were a few instances when I was eager to advance, ready to move on to a new position after just a few months (not a representation of what "good" looks like). I had caught a case of FOMO (fear of missing out). My first career Champion, Paula, assured me that any step taken after underperforming in a job/rotation would be far worse than a mediocre "next step" after excelling in my current role.

The overall goal with the Champion is to have more confidence in properly navigating the waters of the professional voyage. They will help guide our career maps and help us understand how and where we fit into the larger puzzle at our company. We can break this down into the following goals to start:

1. **Strategic Vision:** Collaborate with Champions to discern broader industry landscapes, debate upcoming shifts, and align your career trajectory accordingly.

2. **Holistic Growth:** Harness their deep knowledge to identify skill gaps, gain insights into organizational intricacies, and absorb leadership techniques crucial for your advancement.

3. **Network Expansion:** Through them, you can tap into influential figures in your field, potentially unveiling new avenues of opportunities.

4. **Career Mapping:** Strategize your career paths, starting with your ultimate objectives and working backward. This method ensures every step aligns with your long-term vision.

The text message screenshot below is from Tien, my Champion on my entrepreneurial journey. At times he was a cheerleader for me, especially through tough times. I will never forget this message that he sent. (You might already be familiar with the poem!)

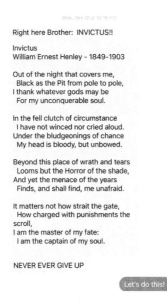

Mon, Oct 12 at 10:16 PM

Right here Brother: INVICTUS!!

Invictus
William Ernest Henley ~ 1849-1903

Out of the night that covers me,
  Black as the Pit from pole to pole,
I thank whatever gods may be
  For my unconquerable soul.

In the fell clutch of circumstance
  I have not winced nor cried aloud.
Under the bludgeonings of chance
  My head is bloody, but unbowed.

Beyond this place of wrath and tears
  Looms but the Horror of the shade,
And yet the menace of the years
  Finds, and shall find, me unafraid.

It matters not how strait the gate,
  How charged with punishments the scroll,
I am the master of my fate:
  I am the captain of my soul.

NEVER EVER GIVE UP

Let's do this!

Figure 51: A motivational text message from Tien, one of my Champions when doubling as a professional cheerleader, pushing me forward.

Frequency of Interaction

You'll likely engage with your Champion on a quarterly basis or perhaps less frequently, depending on their availability. However, their insight, stemming from in-depth experience, renders every interaction invaluable. Ideally, you should meet with them every other month when getting started, and then extend the frequency to quarterly. Try not to let more than four to six months pass without a Champion session!

Contributions to Career Map

You will work with your Champion on the later stages of your career map and then work backward. They have likely interacted with people close to the top of the organization and at most levels throughout, so they'll know what it takes to get to most positions. Think about the second habit covered in Stephen Covey's *7 Habits of Highly Effective People*: "Begin with the end in mind" when working with your champion. What is it that you truly want to achieve? What are options B and C? Then you can start to reverse engineer the map options best suited for you and the corresponding skills, roles, experiences, achievements, and relationships it will take to get there.

Paula was an exceptional Champion during my professional journey. Our interaction started with her as my Functional Mentor and gradually shifted as she ascended in her role and our discussions moved from monthly to quarterly. Paula helped me navigate intricate work situations, assisted me in understanding job requirements, and offered wisdom during times of moral conflict. Her guidance was instrumental in my professional development; she helped me understand how I fit into the larger picture of the organization and what was truly needed for growth and promotion. She helped guide me toward stretch assignments and also acted as a lighthouse, helping me avoid "rocky cliffs" in the form of projects, programs, teams, and people to stay away from. Paula also challenged me to think long and hard about what I truly wanted and what was best for me. This was possible because we built out my full career map early on, and she knew what I wanted in life and where I wanted to be at the end of my professional career.

Conversation Flow

Conversations with your Champion will typically follow the "Board Conversation Flow" in Chapter 9. The details of this section outline various other topics you may discuss throughout the relationship. Try to schedule these sessions for fifty minutes (so you'll always finish ten minutes shy of the hour). The less frequently you meet with your board members, the longer your sessions may need to be. Shaving ten minutes off an hour-long meeting is a considerate way to respect their time and create a buffer for them. It also affords you the opportunity to add three minutes, if absolutely necessary, without making them late for their next meeting.

Conversation 1

- Establish communication norms and understand their communication preferences.

- Determine how they'd prefer to be updated or approached outside of scheduled interactions.

- Prioritize sending an agenda and list of questions at least forty-eight hours before every meeting, allowing them ample reflection time. Let them know that you will be taking the burden of conversation prep and continuity off their plates.

- Share your long-term vision and present our career maps early on in the relationship, highlighting both immediate and distant goals. This offers champions a comprehensive view of your aspirations.

Conversation 2

- Understand their journey on a more intimate level by delving into the challenges they've faced, the strategies they employed, and decisions they might reconsider with the wisdom of hindsight.

- Ask for advice on how your work aligns with the bigger picture at your company by understanding how your current project and team contribute to the organization's broader objectives, mission, and purpose. Seek guidance on how you can align your endeavors for maximum impact.

- Consult your Champion about stretch assignments by discussing potential roles or projects that could challenge you, facilitating growth, and enhancing your professional visibility.

Ongoing Conversations

- Regularly revisit your career trajectory with them, ensuring alignment with the broader organization and industry vision.

- Understand their perception of your growth, areas needing attention, and strategies to remain in tune with organizational and industry evolutions.

- Thank them for their precious time, insights, and perspectives!

"Surround yourself with great people who dream larger than you do, have achieved what you aspire to do, and whom you resonate with personally and professionally—these are the ones that help your right future arrive sooner."

Pete Schramm

What If I No Longer Have Somebody More Than Ten Years Ahead of Me?

For those currently at "the top of the food chain," in a high position, seeking individuals with significantly more experience, this role can be filled by another Accountability Partner, Functional Mentor, or Cross-Functional Mentor. The choice depends on your needs, career stage, and goals. I have also guided high-level executives in engaging members of their company's board to serve as Champions on their own PBAs.

How to Get in Touch with a High-Level Champion Prospect

Identifying and reaching out to a high-level Champion within your organization can feel daunting, but it's a necessary strategic move for your career development. Here are a few steps and tips to consider:

Identify (the Right) Potential Champions: Look for high-level individuals who demonstrate interest in your area of work or who have a history of advocating for others. They might be in your department, or another one, or even in a different branch of the organization. You can find them by observing who speaks up and advocates for others in meetings, who takes the time to mentor and guide people in a role/level similar to yours, or who actively engages in diversity and inclusion initiatives.

Build Your Reputation: Before reaching out, ensure that you have built a strong professional reputation. Your work ethic, contributions, and professionalism should speak for themselves. Champions are more likely to invest their time in and stake their reputation on those they believe have potential and are committed.

Leverage Your Network: If you know someone who can provide a warm introduction, this is often a great approach. They could be a mutual acquaintance, a boss, or a mentor; whoever it is, make sure this person can vouch for your skills and potential. Warm introductions can help establish an initial level of trust and familiarity.

Request an Initial Meeting (Gradually Building Rapport): If a warm introduction isn't possible, craft a respectful, concise, and compelling message via email or a formal letter. Clearly articulate who you are, your purpose for reaching out, and why you believe they would be the ideal Champion for you. Be sure to mention any commonalities that could help establish a connection. Instead of asking for mentorship or sponsorship outright, a better approach is often to ask for a brief meeting. This could be a coffee chat or a short virtual meeting where you can express your admiration for their work and seek advice. Building a relationship with a Champion is not an overnight process. Be patient, consistent, and authentic in your interactions.

Finally, remember that not everyone you approach will agree to be your Champion, and that's okay. It's important to find someone who is the right fit for you and your career aspirations.

What to Avoid

Respect the Champion's time more than that of any other board member. Imagine if you were talking to the CEO of Google—how much would you prepare for that conversation? Are you ready to have someone that important and powerful as a Champion, or should you work with a person one or two levels lower? Resist the temptation to over rely on your Champion, and never expect them to solve problems for you. They are there to guide you and help you make your own decisions. Equally, a Champion should not impose their methods on you; their role is to foster your unique path, not create a duplicate of theirs.

When We Are Champions for Others

Remember that not all protégés are created equal, and taking time to understand the variations across generations is critical when providing guidance to others. Some studies have indicated that younger generations might have higher expectations regarding career progression and workplace benefits compared to older generations.[23] This difference is often attributed to the rapid pace of change they've grown up with, enabled by technology and the digital age.

The modern work environment, with its emphasis on start-ups, gig economies, and entrepreneurial ventures, might have contributed to the perception of faster success and growth. Moreover, social media showcases "overnight successes," which can sometimes skew perceptions. Additionally, many younger employees are driven by a desire for meaningful work and personal growth, rather than just job security.[24] This could translate into a desire for faster progression into roles that they find fulfilling.

Split-level relationships are becoming increasingly important with the aging workforce retiring and the talent gap widening. As a Champion, we can promote transparency "from the top" by involving multiple levels of employees. These meetings also provide a platform for employees at all levels to voice their concerns, suggestions, or ideas, promoting a culture of inclusivity. They allow for more holistic and comprehensive problem-solving, helping employees feel valued and heard.

---

23 Twenge, J. M., and S. M. Campbell. 2008. "Generational Differences in Psychological Traits and Their Impact on the Workplace." *Journal of Managerial Psychology* 23 (8): 862–77.

24 Deal, J. J., D. G. Altman, and S. G. Rogelberg. 2010. Millennials at Work: What We Know and What We Need to Do (If Anything). *Journal of Business and Psychology* 25: 191–9.

Action and Reflection

My Champions have emphasized that time in a role allows for deeper understanding, skill acquisition, and maturity, all of which are invaluable in higher positions. They also reminded me that rapid promotions without gaining essential experience could be detrimental to me and to the organization. Here are some other things to think about as we wrap up Chapter 16:

1. Ask your Champion about stories of successful individuals who took time to build their careers.

2. Ask your Champion what else they suggest for the "end" of your career map based on what you truly want out of life. They may have some other "ends" in mind for you as the relationship deepens.

3. How are you tracking the relationship with your current Champions? This is a great time to hop back onto the companion website to record updates.

4. Take a moment to shoot your Champions an email thanking them for their time and/or sharing a progress update.

Champion	
Seat Details	Strategic Guide and "Split Level Advisor"
Icon Recap	Lighthouse—guide from afar, help navigate the long journey; understand larger picture sooner
Experience	10+ Yrs more and 2 Levels above you
Internal vs. External	Internal
My Goal with Them	Help understand what is possible; how fits into larger puzzle long-term; more strategic industry trends; promotion strategies
Career Map Contributions	Work career map backward (begin with the end in mind); understand what can happen at each stage; add details to Achievement and Accomplishment column
Their Background	Share your values and care about your career aspirations, have proven track record and strong network; ideally some background and future career map steps overlap
Meeting Frequency	Every 3–6 months

Figure 52: Summarizes the Champion details of the PBA Matrix.

Space for your notes and reflection.

CHAPTER 17

ALLY:

THE COLLABORATIVE PARTNER
AND PERSPECTIVE ADVISOR

"Each of us needs all of us."

Ancient Proverb

The concepts in this chapter can be carried out through the other seats on our PBA, even if that specific person is not primarily filling the Ally role for us.

In the sprawling expanse of professional terrains, Allies are akin to binoculars. They enhance our worldview, bringing clarity to perspectives and lived experiences outside of our own. Just as binoculars provide a focused, magnified vision of distant landscapes, Allies offer an enriched understanding of the terrains around us, especially when we identify areas of vulnerability.

Dr. Victoria Mattingly (Dr. V), a leading voice in the diversity, equity, inclusion, and belonging (DEIB) discourse, maintains that being an Ally is a proactive endeavor. It involves engaging with different perspectives and advocating for those perspectives when they're absent. An Ally uses their power, privilege, and status to support and advocate for people who differ from them in some meaningful way. Consider male Allies for women, straight Allies for members of the LGBTQ+ community, and so forth.

Being an Ally isn't just about pledging support; it's about contributing meaningfully to a culture of inclusivity. Dr. V, who has spent years researching allyship and inclusion, defines inclusion as the behaviors that result in others feeling valued, respected, seen, and heard. This outcome should be of utmost concern for Allies, especially when supporting underrepresented and historically disadvantaged groups in the workplace. She tells us that the term "ally" should not be self-proclaimed but rather "awarded" by another person with whom you are engaging.

Embarking on our professional journey, we carry a unique blend of strengths and privileges, along with areas where we might not wield as much power. Some of us might find we're in a unique position where the pressing challenges of discrimination don't weigh upon us as heavily. For instance, if you are a white, cisgender, able-bodied, heterosexual male, you might not immediately feel the need for an Ally—unless, of course, you belong to another marginalized group such as neurodiverse individuals, parents, or veterans. If you do not feel the need for an Ally, consider this chapter as a guide for how you may be an Ally for someone else.

Here are some example scenarios to demonstrate the concept of allyship:

In a Corporate Ladder:

You: *A young female entrepreneur in tech, confronting the hurdles of a male-centric industry*

Your Ally: *A seasoned male executive who recognizes the industry biases and facilitates your learning and professional progress through introductions and insights*

In Academia:

You: *A first-generation college student, new to the nuances of higher education*

Your Ally: *An established professor or elder student who guides you and ensures a smooth integration*

On Social Platforms:

You: *An older introvert seeking a voice in public speaking arenas*

Your Ally: *A younger, influential, charismatic speaker who aids in refining your skills, providing platforms, and instilling confidence*

Are you part of a marginalized identity group? (See the list on the following pages.) Do you find yourself in situations with a power differential where you are not in the seat of power?

Figure 53: The binoculars represent the Ally role on your PBA.

Goals for This Relationship

Your Ally brings together many of the other board seat responsibilities and helps you understand things from various points of view. That is because for someone to be your Ally, they need to be different from you in some significant way. They need to belong to a non-marginalized identity group of power to which you don't belong. They can bring guidance, awareness, perspective, support, and lived experience to your conversations that may otherwise be inaccessible to you. This awareness can then expand your worldview and, as a result, make you better equipped to succeed in an increasingly diverse workplace and society.

Your goals, therefore, are:

- Understand their background and lived experiences.

- Cultivate an understanding of situations from a multifaceted perspective (foreign experiences to you).

- Work with them to complement your vulnerabilities with their strength, ensuring a well-rounded approach to obstacles.

- Share your experiences so they can amplify your voice and ensure it's heard.

- Work together, continuously challenging and correcting any unconscious biases or misperceptions on both sides.

As a tall, white, male there are many things that I take for granted. When I served on someone else's PBA as an Ally, learning about their lived experiences, I was amazed to hear how certain people were treated by others personally, professionally, and legally. My eyes were opened to what I didn't know I didn't

know. The more I asked, the more I learned. It's similar to talking with veterans: sometimes, the best thing we can do is say hello and be there to listen. I hope this chapter helps us all take a big step in the right direction—realizing that our differences can indeed help us form a stronger tomorrow together. We all win more when we get this right!

Recognizing and understanding the following facets of diversity can lead to more inclusive and enriched environments in both professional and personal settings. This is not a book focused on diversity, but I do want to highlight that there are many forms to consider when diversifying our board, and I encourage you to be cognizant of differences in the world overall. Here's a structured breakdown of identity groups, with examples and brief descriptions of each:

Demographic Diversity

1. **Gender**
   - Example: Men, Women, Non-binary, Transgender, Genderqueer
   - Description: Represents the spectrum of genders, beyond just binary male and female.

2. **Racial differences**
   - Example: Caucasian, African American, Asian, Native American
   - Description: Embraces various racial and ethnic backgrounds.

3. **Generations**
   - Example: Baby Boomers, Gen X, Millennials, Gen Z
   - Description: Refers to the distinct generational experiences and worldviews.

4. **Religion**
   - Examples: Christianity, Islam, Hinduism, Atheism, Buddhism, Judaism
   - Description: Recognizes diverse religious beliefs and practices.

5. **Sexual Orientation**
   - Example: Heterosexual, Homosexual, Bisexual, Asexual
   - Description: Encompasses the spectrum of sexual attractions and orientations.

Socioeconomic Diversity

6. Economic Status

- Example: Low-income, Middle-class, Affluent
- Description: Highlights variations in financial backgrounds and current economic conditions.

7. Geographic and Cultural Backgrounds

- Example: Urban Upbringing, Rural Roots, Immigrants, Nomadic Cultures
- Description: Points to diverse geographic origins and cultural influences.

8. Education and Academic Backgrounds

- Example: High School Diploma, Vocational Training, PhD in Physics, Liberal Arts Degree
- Description: Delineates differences in education levels, fields of study, and academic institutions.

Professional & Cognitive Diversity

9. Veteran Status

- Example: Combat Veterans, Noncombat Military Personnel, Reserve Forces
- Description: Acknowledges the varied experiences within military service.

10. Work Experience and Career Path

- Example: Seasoned Professionals, Entry-level Graduates, Career Switchers
- Description: Demonstrates different professional trajectories and industry experiences.

11. Thought Processes

- Example: Analytical Thinkers, Creative Minds, Pragmatic Decision Makers
- Description: Represents variations in thought patterns and decision-making approaches.

Physical & Health Diversity

12. Accessibility

- Examples: Wheelchair Users, Individuals with Hearing Aids, People with Invisible Disabilities

- Description: Encompasses both visible and invisible disabilities.

13. Physical Appearance

- Examples: Tall Individuals, People with Tattoos, Individuals with Albinism

- Description: Recognizes the diversity in physical attributes and appearances.

14. Health Status

- Examples: Individuals with Diabetes, Cancer Survivors, People Living with HIV

- Description: Reveals differences in health conditions and chronic illnesses.

Personal & Lifestyle Diversity

15. Marital and Family Status

- Examples: Single Parents, Child-Free Couples, Multi-generational Households

- Description: Differentiates family structures and marital statuses.

16. Hobbies and Interests

- Examples: Amateur Astronomers, Ballroom Dancers, Vintage Car Enthusiasts

- Description: Categorizes diverse personal interests and hobbies that shape unique perspectives.

17. Life Experiences

- Examples: Refugees, World Travelers, Individuals Who've Overcome Addiction

- Description: Shows distinct life events and experiences that mold individual worldviews.

18. Socio-political Beliefs

- Example: Progressives, Conservatives, Libertarians, Activists
- Description: Delineates diverse political ideologies and levels of civic engagement.

19. Neurodiversity Spectrum

- Example: Individuals with Autism, ADHD, Dyslexia
- Description: Recognizes the spectrum of neurological differences.

20. Language and Communication Styles

- Example: Multilingual Speakers, Sign Language Users, Verbose Communicators
- Description: Presents different native languages, dialects, and preferences in communication.

"It's our differences that can bring us together and help open our eyes to more aspects of each situation—when we give it the chance, together."

- Pete Schramm

Frequency of Interaction

The frequency of Ally conversations will vary drastically across PBAs and will likely be more frequent at the start of the relationship. Meet twice monthly for the first two to three months and then once monthly for the next nine months (completing a full one-year cycle). You may have multiple Allies as you progress in your journey.

Contributions to Career Map

Your Ally (or Allies) will help you in reviewing all aspects of your career map and will work with you in reflecting on previous accomplishments. This role may be at any level in the organization, and you will likely have an external Ally at some point to bring additional perspective—I love it when this happens! It is helpful to discuss their career maps and learn about their experiences (good and bad) as well. Similar to the Sponsor, the Ally can help build you up and bring you into conversations and situations in which you may have been overlooked or forgotten in the past.

Conversation Flow

Ally conversations will typically follow the "Board Conversation Flow" in Chapter 9. The details of this section outline some of the other topics you may address throughout the relationship.

Conversation 1

- Learn about their background and journey.
- Review the in-play topics and the out-of-play topics (boundaries).
- Talk about what diversity means to each of you.

Conversation 2

- Share your recent experiences with inclusion gone right or gone wrong.
- What have you done since your last conversation to think of alternative perspectives in situations?
- How have you supported inclusion in action?

Conversation 3

- Compare personal boards and career maps.
- Are there any specific opportunities that you can explore to learn more about DEIB?

Dr. V emphasizes the importance of distinguishing between "Big A" Allyship and "Little a" allyship. "Big A" Allyship refers to larger steps like sponsoring and activism, while "Little a" allyship involves smaller, more personal gestures like inviting others in and being intentional about microaffirmations. You may have heard of microaggressions—small actions, such as interrupting someone or questioning their judgment, that can make people feel uncomfortable or dismissed. Microaffirmations, on the other hand, are subtle but positive actions that make individuals feel seen and supported.

What to Be Aware of When You Are the Ally

This section places you in the Ally seat, leveraging your own privilege/power on behalf of those in a position of less power or who are underrepresented. One of the most common pitfalls for those seeking to serve as an Ally to a Partner (the person receiving the Ally's support) is tokenism. This refers to the practice of making superficial efforts to be inclusive, merely to give the appearance of diversity. In the context of your PBA, this might manifest as selecting someone purely based on their identity group, without genuinely valuing their unique experiences and insights.

You might be tokenizing someone if:

- Your primary or sole reason for bringing you onto their PBA is to "check a box" for diversity.
- You're not genuinely interested in or open to their perspectives, especially if they challenge your existing beliefs.
- You sideline or diminish their opinions in discussions, consciously or unconsciously.

Engaging with an Ally or Partner from a different background can be uncomfortable, especially if we're not used to discussing issues related to diversity, equity, and inclusion. To overcome this:

- Acknowledge the discomfort and understand that it's a natural part of growth.
- Educate yourself. Read, attend workshops, or engage in discussions about diversity and inclusion to become more familiar with various perspectives.
- Approach the relationship with humility. It's OK not to have all the answers; be open to learning from your Ally.

To avoid tokenism and foster a genuine relationship with your Partner/Ally:

- Engage with them as a whole person, not just a representative of a particular identity group.
- Be genuinely curious. Ask open-ended questions and listen actively to their answers.
- Seek feedback. Regularly check in with your Partner/Ally to ensure the relationship feels mutually beneficial and respectful.
- Reflect on your motives. Periodically reassess why you sought an Ally in the first place. Ensure it's for genuine growth and not just to appear inclusive.

Remember, the goal of having an Ally on our PBA is not just to ask for a "handout" and diversify the board in appearance but to genuinely broaden your perspectives and challenge your beliefs. It's about building meaningful, respectful relationships that enrich both parties involved.

Melinda Epler, in her actionable TED Talk "Be An Ally," underscores that systemic change in diversity and inclusion is an incremental process. It necessitates individual actions, words, and gestures. An Ally amplifies these efforts, promoting a more inclusive environment.

Drawing inspiration from Epler's insights, we can think through a few ways to put this into action:

1. *Constantly educate ourselves about the challenges faced by marginalized groups. Reflect on our inherent biases and actively work to rectify them.*

2. *Whenever we notice discrimination or microaggressions, speak up. Amplify the voices of marginalized people in spaces where they might not be heard.*

3. *Offer support, both emotional and tangible. Advocate for equal opportunities and be a voice for change.*

Action and Reflection

The journey doesn't stop at seeking an Ally for your PBA. In areas where you hold power and privilege, you can serve as an Ally for someone else. Offer them the clarity, support, and understanding they seek. Sometimes, the most impactful change we can make is to use our positions of privilege to uplift others.

We covered a lot in this chapter. It may be helpful to go for a walk, take a few extra notes, or read through the thoughts below to decide what actions or reflections matter most at this time.

1. Where do you currently stand in your understanding and appreciation of diversity, equity, inclusion, and belonging? How might the unique perspectives of an Ally enhance and broaden your worldview?

2. Think about your current professional and personal networks. Are there individuals who come from backgrounds or identity groups distinctly different from your own? How might they offer a fresh perspective and challenge your current beliefs?

3. Reflect on past interactions where someone acted as an Ally to you. Were their actions more in line with "Big A" or "Little a" allyship? What kind of Ally would be most beneficial for your PBA?

4. While the chapter emphasizes finding an Ally for your PBA, how can you ensure that the relationship is mutually beneficial and not one-sided?

5. Forming a relationship with an Ally, especially one centered around sensitive topics like diversity, can be challenging. What potential challenges do you anticipate in building this relationship, and how can you preemptively address them to foster genuine understanding and trust?

Ally	
Seat Details	Collaborative Partner and Perspective Advisor
Icon Recap	Binoculars—enhance world view, bring perspective and clarity; have lived experiences outside of yours
Experience	Your choice in age and experience
Internal vs. External	Internal (can be external if you work at a smaller company)
My Goal with Them	Diversify perspective, build inclusivity, guide on how to handle prejudice and discrimination and build bridges together; partner in journey, ensure your path is navigated with wisdom, support, and empathy
Career Map Contributions	Review each others' career maps; understand differences in paths taken and plans for the future; help each other reach deserved positions, not what bucket others put you in
Their Background	Will come from a different identity group and a stronger position with influence or power; not under-represented in an area you are
Meeting Frequency	Monthly

Figure 54: Summarizes the Ally details of the PBA Matrix.

Space for your notes and reflection.

CHAPTER 18

SUPERVISOR/MANAGER:

YOUR BOSS AND DAILY ADVISOR

"A good boss makes their people realize
they have more ability than they think they have
so that they consistently do better work than they
thought they could."

Charles Erwin Wilson, American engineer and businessman
who served as the CEO of General Motors during World War II
and then went on to serve as the Secretary of Defense

Among the limitless and unpredictable ocean of our professional journey, if our career is the ship, then the Supervisor or Manager serves as its helm or steering wheel, directing its course and ensuring its alignment with the desired destination. They not only help navigate through calm waters but also guide the ship safely through storms and rough seas. The role of a Supervisor is not just to supervise but to lead, guide, and, most importantly, steer employees toward success. They are instrumental in identifying the latent strengths in their team members, addressing areas of improvement, and paving the way for them to achieve their career aspirations. Through a balance of constructive feedback and encouragement, they champion continuous learning and usher in opportunities for both personal and professional growth.

Great supervisors can seem like superheroes while bad bosses are akin to a "super-zero."

Supervisors and Managers have a profound impact on their team's professional growth. They aren't just taskmasters but nurturers of talent and potential. Their role extends beyond overseeing daily tasks to actively engaging in mentoring, offering feedback, and ensuring a conducive work environment for their team members to thrive.

Maribeth was one of my favorite leaders to work for. She called me out on my areas for improvement, and she helped amplify the wins that I had. Our interactions were more than just professional check-ins; they were sessions of mutual growth, feedback, and vision alignment. With her guidance, I felt not only directed but also empowered. We had 7 a.m. coffee in her office (after a fifty-minute drive from my apartment in Virginia), and she would provide feedback to me there, first asking if I had any takeaways or thoughts on a recent meeting, project, or interaction. She never belittled me; never punished me in public; and always ended our chats with a matrix of what we had done, what we planned to do, and how professional growth ought to continue!

Conversely, I recall a previous Manager of mine who never had time for one-on-ones, never had time for discussions about my career development, and never had time for me to ask questions or request feedback. I did not last long in that role, and I spent much more time with my budding PBA during this chapter of my life. These concepts will be highlighted in more detail in the "what to avoid" section at the end of this chapter.

This board seat is treated differently from the others, where you invite someone to sit on your board. No one I've ever met had total say in choosing some of their early career Supervisors! Yet, you want to have them on your PBA for that reason. When we change jobs and get a new Manager, this role is refilled by the new Manager, and we then have the option to "hire" the old Manager onto our PBA to fill another seat (where it makes sense). You may also decide to keep the old Manager on your "PBA bench" and stay in touch with them over time, keeping the relationship warm for when some PBA "rewiring" takes place.

Figure 55:The helm (ship steering wheel) represents the Supervisor/Manager role on your PBA.

Goals for This Relationship

Gallup, McKinsey & Company, *Harvard Business Review*, *Forbes*, and other reputable leadership outlets continue to share that one of the biggest reasons why employees leave companies is poor relationships with the people they work with. Usually, the Manager/Supervisor is the most responsible for these departures. For this reason, I also call the Manager/Supervisor board seat the "make it or break it" advisor. When we do the hard work early of building a strong relationship with our Manager, we can avoid some of these pitfalls and mishaps. Remember that not all bosses are created equal, so at times we need to help guide them toward what is truly needed most and how to be good at this professional development thing!

We always want to keep a professional relationship with our Manager and to be clear about boundaries for work hours, topics discussed, how to give/review feedback, expectations, and priorities.

1. **Establish Clear Communication** and ensure alignment on roles, responsibilities, and expectations.

2. **Create a Development Plan** to align on professional growth, skill enhancement, and future aspirations. Think of this as the precareer-map process.

3. **Ensure Resource Availability** and make it clear when you do and do not have the necessary tools, environment, and support to excel.

4. **Understand Performance Review Processes** to gain clarity on evaluation criteria and timelines.

5. **Set Up Feedback Mechanisms** and engage in regular check-ins to discuss performance and growth areas. You may like to use the start-stop-continue-shift methodology (highlighted in Chapter 9) for your one-on-one and feedback sessions.

Frequency of Interaction

For early-career professionals, frequent check-ins are crucial. At this stage, you are typically in a phase of intensive learning and skill acquisition. A study from the *Harvard Business Review* suggests that younger professionals, especially those in the Millennial and Gen Z cohorts, value consistent feedback and mentorship.[25] Weekly informal interactions, coupled with biweekly structured discussions, can be extremely valuable.

As you progress to the midcareer stage, the need for guidance reduces, but the importance of strategic alignment and professional growth becomes paramount. Monthly or bimonthly structured meetings can be more appropriate to focus on career development, project alignment, and long-term goals.[26] Weekly touch points for work that needs to be done are still strongly encouraged.

As you reach the end stages of your career, the emphasis often shifts toward strategic direction, mentoring junior colleagues, and succession planning. Quarterly in-depth reviews, along with more frequent informal interactions, might be the ideal cadence. At this stage, the dialogue often becomes more bidirectional, with both you and your superior learning from one another.[27]

Contributions to Career Map

"Leaders become great not because of their power, but because of their ability to empower others."

John Maxwell, an internationally recognized speaker and author on leadership and professional development

Schedule time every month to review your goals and progress toward the metrics by which you'll be evaluated at your performance review. These check-ins are essential for tracking progress, addressing issues, and adjusting goals as necessary. Your Manager should contribute to your career map by identifying opportunities for growth, suggesting resources for learning, and providing guidance and support.

---

25 Meister, J.C. and K. Willyerd. 2010. "Mentoring Millennials." *Harvard Business Review.*

26 Corporate Executive Board. 2011. "Driving Performance and Retention Through Employee Engagement."

27 Ibarra, H. 2015. *Act Like a Leader, Think Like a Leader.* Harvard Business Review Press.

Conversation Flow

Conversations with your Supervisor/Manager will typically follow the "Board Conversation Flow" in Chapter 9. This section goes into more detail due to the unique relationship and power dynamic.

Initial Interactions

- Lay a foundation that facilitates future communication and mutual understanding. Begin by discussing your career aspirations, setting initial professional development goals, and establishing clear expectations.

- Share more about your background and show genuine interest by inquiring about their hobbies or what they do for fun.

- Ask about the traits or actions of their previously super successful employees and what made them so valuable.

- Share experiences about your previous bosses and elaborate on what worked and what didn't, to give your Supervisor an understanding of your past professional landscape and preferences.

Conversation 1

- Emphasize clear communication of priorities, ensuring that you both align in terms of support, contribution, and mission. This is where you delve into the "why" before discussing the "how" and the "what."

- Share your progress toward the goals you've set. This discussion—and those that follow—should be marked by openness, honesty, mutual respect, and constructive feedback.

Conversation 2

- Confirm that your expectations align and ensure that you have all the necessary resources to execute your role effectively.

- Discuss any challenges you're facing and keep this topic open for future conversations.

- Establish goal-setting rhythms and begin creating a development plan in collaboration with your Manager.

- Dive into your interests and skills, ensuring you're being used to your full potential. Remember, your Manager might not be aware of all of your capabilities, so it's up to you to communicate your value effectively.

Ongoing Conversations

- Focus on continuous professional development.

- Discuss opportunities for upskilling, reskilling, or acquiring new skills, whether through classes, certifications, or conferences.

- Ask about the benchmarks for top performance ratings. If a leader tells you "Nobody ever gets a 5," challenge that notion. Seek clarity. Understand what excellence looks like in their eyes. Often, it might revolve around creating a transformative tool, improving a process, or achieving something that benefits a broader audience within the organization.

- Review your job description; if you find your responsibilities have outgrown it, perhaps it's time to reconsider your role or even explore promotional opportunities.

I began to share the story of a previous Supervisor, Kim, in Chapter 13: Functional Mentor. I refer to her as a Supervisor, not a manager or boss, because she truly had a super impact on my life. I received advice to gain profit and loss (P&L) experience while in my Senior Quality Engineering function if I aspired to leadership, particularly aiming for a program manager role. I reviewed my career map with Kim, my Supervisor, early in our collaboration, and she assisted me in identifying stretch assignments (i.e., tasks beyond my regular duties). This work didn't mean extra pay, and I often had to complete these projects outside my standard working hours. Kim supported me in obtaining the necessary training and applying those newly acquired P&L skills in real-world projects. We continually refined my career map, and I also learned about her goals and aspirations. After a few years, we identified a program manager position (outside her team) that seemed a perfect fit for me. I applied and was eventually hired, making it one of the most challenging roles to depart from due to the incredible team. Despite her preference for a rival football team, Kim holds the title of "best boss ever" in my heart. She equipped me with valuable tools that proved instrumental when I launched and expanded my own business—nearly a decade later!

What to Avoid

When engaging in conversations about professional growth with your Supervisor, it's essential to navigate the discussion with tact and clarity. Avoid lapses in conversation that can lead to misunderstandings about expectations and priorities. Instead, strive for transparency, ensuring that you both are on the same page regarding your goals and the roadmap to achieve them. Also, while it's crucial to be open about your aspirations, be wary of setting unrealistic expectations that might set you up for disappointment.

Trust plays a significant role in these discussions. Actions that erode trust, such as taking undue credit, failing to acknowledge contributions, or not living up to commitments, can hinder the open flow of dialogue. It's equally vital to respect boundaries, ensuring that the relationship remains professional. Avoid delving into personal territories unless they are relevant to the discussion at hand. Lastly, always remember that these conversations are a two-way street. While the relationship is predominantly meant to support your growth, understanding your Manager's perspective and constraints will lead to more productive and fruitful discussions.

> *"A boss should be a mentor, a leader, and a source of guidance, inspiring their employees to reach their full potential."*
>
> *Simon Sinek, a globally known author and speaker, the father of "start with why," and a distant, peripheral Champion to me*

If You Don't Have a Boss (#entrepreneur)

The prospect of "no longer having a boss" has become increasingly attractive, with the rate of new entrepreneurs rising by eight percent from 2019 to 2020 alone, as reported by Forbes. In fact, as I write this book, I technically do not have a boss! As entrepreneurs, we have the option to add another Accountability Partner, a cofounder, or perhaps a corporate board member or an investor to this board seat. Many of the principles surrounding goal setting, performance reviews, accountability, and feedback stay consistent.

When We Are the Supervisor

Don't suck! Stepping into leadership means embodying the work ethic and attitude you wish to instill in your team. Leading by example, coupled with clear and honest communication, builds trust and fosters a collaborative environment. Every member of your team, regardless of rank or tenure, deserves respect and acknowledgment for their contributions. Providing them with the necessary resources and guidance is paramount. Celebrate their achievements and understand what motivates each individual. For younger team members with exceptional skills, consider early promotions. Conversely, appreciate experienced team members for the quality of their work, not just the hours they clock.

Meanwhile, there are several pitfalls to avoid. Promising promotions or raises without following through can deeply erode trust. Employees also need to feel safe; creating an environment where they fear speaking up stifles growth and innovation. Avoid being overly directive; employees should understand the reasons behind tasks. Ignoring or neglecting feedback can lead to missed growth opportunities. Additionally, showing favoritism can demotivate deserving employees and sour the team dynamic. Regularly reflect on your team's achievements and plan for future growth to ensure you remain a proactive and respected leader.

Action and Reflection

As we wrap up Chapter 18, start to think about what you can be doing today and what you may already be doing but just not tracking ... yet!

1. Is your Supervisor currently sitting on multiple board seats on your PBA? Can you reduce risk and single points of failure by keeping them in just one seat and finding another person for the duplicative spots?

2. When was the last time that you asked your Supervisor for suggestions regarding people to fill seats on your PBA?

3. How often do you review and update your career map with your Supervisor?

4. When was the last time you talked through your Supervisor's career map?

Supervisor/Manager	
Seat Details	Your Boss and Daily Advisor
Icon Recap	Ship's Helm (steering wheel)—guide daily work; closest to professional development
Experience	Will vary; don't usually get to choose
Internal vs. External	Internal—(if entrepreneur, may be filled by others: advisor, investor, Champion, another Mentor)
My Goal with Them	Excel in your role, know what is expected, understand performance reviews, goal setting, filling out board with people they suggest
Career Map Contributions	Help understand how current role can build into next; help work on projects and tasks aligned with future roles on career map
Their Background	Will vary; don't usually get to choose
Meeting Frequency	Weekly (live or asynchronous); structure may adjust to every other week then to monthly

Figure 56: Summarizes the Supervisor/Manager details of the PBA Matrix.

CHAPTER 19:

SUCCESSOR:

THE PROTÉGÉ-IN-TRAINING
AND REVERSE MENTOR

*"In learning, you will teach, and in teaching,
you will learn."*

*Phil Collins, an amazing singer, and songwriter who developed
music that got me and other members of my PBA through
some rough times in the office*

As we ascend the ranks in our professional journey, the notion of a Successor becomes increasingly paramount. However this isn't about mere replacement; it's about shaping a future leader, sculpting their skills, and preparing them to navigate the nuanced labyrinth of our role with dexterity.

Represented by the emblematic captain's hat, the Successor is more than just a prospective employee. This icon, typically donned by those in command, symbolizes the helm of responsibility for which they're being primed. Like the captain's hat, which epitomizes experience, authority, and direction, a Successor is a beacon of an organization's future leadership and vision.

In this expansive ocean of professional evolution, our Successor is the emerging navigator, standing at the brink, ready to take the helm. Through the PBA framework, we don't merely identify this individual but actively mold them, ensuring they're not just replacements but rightful heirs to our legacy.

Yet, are we adequately prepared to pass on this legacy? Have we mapped out processes, solidified relationships, and jotted down invaluable lessons that will help them on their journey? The Successor is poised to absorb and learn, but the onus is on us to impart that wisdom.

This relationship is distinct from other board seats in that while other mentors offer *us* broad guidance and wisdom, the Successor's relationship is deeply tactical, with the flow of information meant to benefit *them*. We must delve into the intricate details of our role, unspoken organizational codes, nurtured relationships, and hard-won challenges. It's a mentorship, yes, but it's also a relay, a passing of a torch that burns with years of experience.

Key Traits of an Ideal Successor

This section was added because of this unique board seat. Our Successor will carry on our work and, perhaps, our legacy in some instances. Understanding key traits and behaviors early on is paramount for a successful "Successor-Successee" relationship. Whether you're in a corporate environment or helming your own entrepreneurial enterprise, the traits you'll want to seek in a Successor remain universally relevant:

Relevant Experience: It's essential for the Successor to have a background that aligns with the role's core duties, even if it doesn't mirror your own trajectory.

Adaptability: In our ever-evolving professional landscape, the ability to pivot and adapt is priceless.

Interpersonal Skills: Given that they'll inherit relationships nurtured over the years, outstanding communication and relationship-building aptitudes are pivotal.

Figure 57: The captain hat represents the Successor role on your PBA.

Goals for This Relationship

In crafting a meaningful relationship with a Successor, the primary aim is to facilitate a seamless transfer of institutional knowledge. This goes beyond merely delineating responsibilities; it's about delving into the intricacies, challenges, and opportunities inherent in the role. As mentors, our objective is to foster the professional growth of the Successor, ensuring they not only adapt to their new role but also thrive within it. However, this relationship is far from one-sided. Embracing the principles of reverse mentorship, we must remain open to the fresh insights and perspectives our Successors bring to the table. Often hailing from a younger generation, they can help uncover for us emerging trends and technologies, creating a symbiotic dynamic where both parties benefit and grow.

Frequency of Interaction

The frequency of interaction with a Successor is often a reflection of the succession plan's maturity and, in some cases, might be predetermined. However, if you find yourself charting this course, it's advisable to commence with weekly interactions, especially at the outset. This initial frequency allows you to rapidly establish rapport and kickstart knowledge transfer. Inviting the Successor to join relevant meetings, both with your current team and external stakeholders, can be particularly beneficial. As you transition into the intermediate phase of the relationship, monthly check-ins become more fitting. These interactions serve as touch points to monitor progress, tackle any emerging challenges, and make any necessary recalibrations. As the baton pass draws near, it's prudent to ramp up your interactions again. This ensures that all preparations are in place and the Successor is poised to step into their new role confidently and competently.

Contributions to Career Map

The Successor will not be as much of a guide on your future career-mapping efforts as other board members; instead, they will benefit from what you have previously done on your career map and will fill the next role on their career map with the role you are currently filling. As a result, it is most helpful to review the four work-related columns on your career map with your Successor. Compare your background to theirs and see if they already have some of the transferable skills and necessary accomplishments "in the bag" in order to hit the ground running. You likely did your homework before you selected them to be your Successor, but the career map comparison can help a lot!

Conversation Flow

Successor conversations will initially follow the "Board Conversation Flow" in Chapter 9. This section is more descriptive of the conversation flow because this role is more about handing off knowledge rather than guiding as much.

During the initial meeting, it's essential for the current role-holder to share their professional journey, highlighting their experiences, challenges faced, and insights into the organization's culture. By doing this, you not only offer a glimpse into the past but also align visions for the future.

Conversation 1

- Dive deep into the intricacies of the role, sharing your personal experiences and the strategies you've adopted over the years.

- Understand the Successor's past experiences, especially challenges they've faced when transitioning into new roles.

- Provide real-time feedback, especially employing methods like start-stop-continue-shift, can provide clarity and direction for both parties.

Conversation 2

- Elaborate on the key supporters, stakeholders (internal and external), and shed light on potential challenges on the horizon.

- Delve into past relationships, especially those that might have gone south, offering insights that can be valuable for the Successor. This discussion isn't just about names and roles but about the dynamics of these relationships.

- Provide the Successor with a comprehensive roadmap to the organization's interpersonal ecosystem.

Ongoing Conversations

- Discuss progress on their career map and uncover experience gaps.

- Explore strategies for work-life balance.

What to Avoid

Successful succession planning is crucial for the smooth transition of roles and responsibilities within an organization. Rather than being a last-minute response to an imminent departure, it should be approached as a strategic initiative and thoughtfully integrated into the broader talent management and leadership development frameworks of the organization. One crucial often overlooked aspect is the value of diversity and inclusion in this process. By ensuring a diverse pipeline of potential Successors, organizations can harness a broader range of perspectives and skills.

Timely identification and preparation of Successors are essential. Delayed or inadequate preparation can hinder the Successor's ability to adapt effectively, potentially leading to disruptions in business continuity. Succession planning should prioritize transparency, with clear communication being paramount. Every stakeholder should be aware of the progress and timeline—from you, as the current role-holder. This transparency not only facilitates smoother transitions but also fosters trust within the organization.

However, even the best-laid plans can go astray without a realistic understanding of the role's demands. Successors should be provided with the necessary resources and support, ensuring they aren't simply "thrown into the deep end." Moreover, understanding the cultural dynamics of the organization is vital. Without this cultural alignment, friction can arise, disrupting the succession process and potentially undermining the Successor's effectiveness in their new role.

When We Are the Successor: Embracing Reverse Mentorship

As we climb the professional ladder, we often find ourselves stepping into roles previously occupied by others. This journey of succession, while rewarding, can span years, with each phase bringing new challenges and learning opportunities. Throughout the journey, it's essential to approach each experience with an open mind and a thirst for knowledge.

The incumbent leader, with their years of experience and deep-rooted organizational understanding, can be an invaluable guide. Their mentorship, combined with training sessions and self-driven learning initiatives, can accelerate our adaptation to the new role. However, this relationship shouldn't be one-sided. As Successors, we shouldn't merely see ourselves as sponges absorbing knowledge. We bring our own unique perspectives, skills, and experiences to the table. Embracing the concept of reverse mentorship allows us to acknowledge that while we're learning from our predecessors, we also have insights and knowledge to share that can enrich the relationship.

Feedback, both giving and receiving, plays a pivotal role in this journey. Constructive feedback helps identify strengths and areas of improvement, ensuring a continuous learning trajectory. Building relationships across the organization, understanding its cultural dynamics, and keeping abreast of changes in the business environment are vital. It's important to remember that while we learn from our predecessors, we're not expected to mirror them. Our leadership style will, and should, evolve based on our individuality.

As we progress in our roles, the weight of our decisions grows, often having far-reaching implications. This underscores the importance of ethical decision-making. And, amidst all the professional challenges, it's crucial to prioritize self-care, ensuring our mental and physical well-being.

Reflecting on my own professional journey, I can attest to the value of proactive succession planning. Regularly updating and reflecting on my experiences not only facilitated my own transitions but also proved instrumental in equipping my Successors for success.

I have prepared a Successor nearly a dozen times in my professional career and start proactively developing a list of "succession planning" documents, beginning with my onboarding process. (Oftentimes, there was nothing in place for onboarding when I transitioned into a role, let alone offboarding!) Document everything you can. I have a monthly reminder in my calendar to review and update the succession documentation. When I worked in corporate America, I tended to schedule this at the same time as I updated my performance review progress (even though performance review updates were only required annually). I passed off this trick to some of my mentees, and they "wowed" some of their new bosses by bringing innovation with them on day one!

Action and Reflection

As we wrap up Chapter 19, start to think about what you can be doing today and what you are maybe already doing but just not tracking . . . yet!

1. Are you just moving forward, or are you paving the way for those who come after you?

2. What can you do right now in your current role (no matter the level) to prepare for your Successor? Would it be valuable to start drafting an "onboarding process" for your position and laying out the details that you likely take for granted?

Successor	
Seat Details	Protege-in-Training and Reverse Mentor
Icon Recap	Captain's Hat—represents passing of the torch and the transition of leadership and responsibility
Experience	5+ Yrs professional in-network (rarely without professional experience)
Internal vs. External	Internal
My Goal with Them	Guide, teach, hand-off role-specific knowledge, skills, and opportunities
Career Map Contributions	Next Steps—how roles contribute to long-term career mapping and the importance of developing a pipeline for future success
Their Background	Aligned with your recent roles and their future career map future roles; focus on completing next future row on their career map
Meeting Frequency	Twice monthly to start, will vary over time; monthly structured conversations

Figure 58: Summarizes the Successor details of the PBA Matrix.

Space for your notes and reflection.

PART

MANAGING YOUR PERSONAL BOARD OF ADVISORS

You now know the who, what, when, where, why, and how of personal boards and career mapping. Part III is geared toward sustaining growth and taking your professional development journey to the next level.

The following chapters will build on the concepts highlighted in Parts I and II, helping you amplify the value of your personal board and optimize your career journey. We'll dive into self-development for maximized board success, explore ethical considerations and diversity on your board, discuss the rest of the -iring process, and delve into board retreats. We finish up by talking about additional resources at your disposal and how to incorporate this methodology into your organization.

CHAPTER 20:

MANAGING (AND DEVELOPING) YOURSELF TO EFFECTIVELY MANAGE YOUR BOARD

"The only person you are destined to become is the person you decide to be."

Ralph Waldo Emerson, a renowned American essayist, lecturer, and poet, known for his influential essays and writings on transcendentalism and individualism

Embarking on a professional journey with your PBA isn't just about them guiding you. It's equally about how you navigate the process, ensuring that you're equipped to absorb, apply, and communicate effectively. This chapter takes us on a journey through communication practices and feedback exercises and lays the groundwork for self-improvement to make the most of our PBA over time.

Mastering Effective Communication

> *"Effective communication is 20% what you know and 80% how you feel about what you know."*
>
> *Jim Rohn, a renowned motivational speaker, entrepreneur, and author*

To maximize the value of your PBA interactions, honing your communication skills is paramount. Work on expressing your thoughts clearly and succinctly, enabling you to communicate your challenges and aspirations effectively to your board members. Can you break each of your thoughts into three bullet points? I've found this trick particularly helpful in improving my brevity. Consider what you are about to say or write, and ask yourself if it can be clearly understood, if outside context is required, and if the receiver of this information will have any follow-up questions.

When you're on the receiving end, developing active listening skills, maintaining eye contact, paraphrasing what the speaker has said, and asking clarifying questions can greatly enhance your understanding and assimilation of their advice. A few clarifying questions to add to your toolbox include:

General Understanding
- Can you elaborate on that point a bit more?
- What do you mean when you say ...?
- Can you give me an example to illustrate that?

Contextual Clarification
- Were there specific circumstances or contexts where you found this to be especially true?
- How does this relate to my current situation or the challenges I've described?

Application and Action
- How might I apply this advice in my current role or project?
- What steps would you suggest I take based on what you've shared?

Source and Reference
- Is there a book, article, or resource where I can learn more about this?
- Who else do you think I should speak to about this topic?

Anticipating Challenges

- What potential obstacles might I encounter if I follow this path?

- Are there common pitfalls or mistakes others make in this situation that I should be aware of?

Easing Into the Feedback Process

Begin with Less Intense Topics: If you're hesitant, start with feedback areas that are less likely to be contentious. This helps in building confidence.

Practice with Trusted Individuals: Before giving or seeking feedback in a professional setting, practice with a trusted friend or mentor.

Self-Reflection First: Before receiving feedback, conduct a self-assessment. This prepares you for potential areas of improvement others might highlight.

Reframe Feedback as a Learning Tool: See feedback as a mechanism for growth, not judgment. This mindset shift can significantly reduce fear.

Repeat Affirmations: Remind yourself that feedback, whether giving or receiving, is an avenue for progress. Positive self-talk can help combat apprehensions.

Facing the Fear in Feedback

Giving and receiving feedback can be tricky. While feedback is an invaluable tool for catalyzing personal and professional growth, it can sometimes feel daunting. To navigate this intricate terrain, let's understand how to ensure feedback remains constructive, focused, and, above all, fearlessly approached.

Jackie, a fellow entrepreneur and friend, follows these five steps for giving feedback:

1. **Ask permission before jumping straight into a feedback session.** Both of us will pause in the conversation and literally ask, "Are you open to some feedback?" The answer can be "no," and in those instances it's best to make note of your piece of feedback for later. When Jackie says "yes," I ask how she would like to receive the feedback.

2. **Be specific and think about how you would receive the feedback** if you were in the receiver's shoes. Jackie brings specific, often real-time examples from a point we just covered in our chat a few moments earlier. When I'm offering feedback, I ask myself: What do I want Jackie to think or do as a result of receiving this feedback? Is it helpful to her or am I merely airing a grievance to feel better?

3. **Balance positivity with constructive criticism** using the velvet brick or feedback sandwich methodology. The velvet brick approach starts with a positive comment about the thought or action and then goes into how that scenario could have played out better (i.e., constructive feedback). The feedback sandwich involves positive, then goes into the constructive piece, and then ends with more positivity related to how the end result could be good in the future now that the receiver is armed with this information.

4. **Lead with empathy** and ensure feedback stems from a desire to support, not to criticize or belittle.

5. **Follow up and touch base in the next scheduled conversation** to ascertain how the feedback has been received and applied. Jackie and I actually take notes on this, and we build it into our agenda for each conversation.

One of my Managers, Daniel, taught me about the equation for receiving feedback, which, when done right, can accelerate professional growth and help the feedback receiver come off as more coachable. I asked Daniel for feedback proactively during our regularly scheduled reviews and at the conclusion of projects and milestones to dive into areas ripe for refinement. Here's the method:

1. **Seek feedback.** I asked Daniel for feedback at the end of each of our one-on-ones. Just like with Jackie, I would share this as an agenda item in advance so he could properly prepare and gather his thoughts.

2. **Listen actively and welcome the feedback.** As an opportunity for growth. Do your best to keep an open mind. The feedback-giver is not an adversary!

3. **Ask clarifying questions.** After Daniel completed a thought, I asked him to delve deeper into any ambiguous areas so I could fully understand the feedback's intent.

4. **Review and reflect.** Sometimes I was not ready to ask clarifying questions on the spot, so I would ask Daniel if I could take time to process what he had said and review it with him later. I then took time to digest the feedback, discerning its relevance and merit before reacting.

5. **Maintain an attitude of gratitude.** Daniel took the time to plan out this feedback and cared enough about my growth to share this with me, so I always appreciated his initiative. Taking a grateful approach nurtures an environment conducive to open dialogue.

6. **Plan to take action!** Before we concluded a feedback conversation, Daniel and I worked together to map out a few actions I could take based on the feedback. Identify specific tasks to be completed by a certain date and agree on how progress will be shared.

Pointers for Avoiding Feedback Pitfalls

When engaging in feedback sessions, it's crucial to allocate adequate time. Rushed feedback often skims the surface, potentially missing deeper issues or nuances. Likewise, interruptions can disrupt the flow of the conversation, so ensure each party has uninterrupted speaking time.

It's also essential to ensure that both parties are in a receptive state of mind. Maintaining privacy during these discussions upholds the dignity of the individual, fostering a more open and honest exchange. Additionally, delivering feedback during high-stress moments rarely facilitates growth; instead, it might intensify tensions. Wait for a calm moment when everyone can maintain a clear head.

Feedback should be rooted in observed behaviors and events; steer clear of rumors or unverified information. It's also vital to avoid overgeneralizing. Accusatory phrases like "you always" or "you never" can create defensiveness, hindering constructive dialogue.

In a single session, it's beneficial to focus on a few main points, ensuring the feedback remains digestible and actionable. Lastly, remember that every individual's journey is unique. Comparing one person to another can be counterproductive and may overshadow the specific feedback's intent.

Role-Playing and Testing Conversations

Practicing role-play with individuals in your network is an excellent way to prepare for upcoming conversations with your PBA. Much like a sales professional prepares for presentations, rehearsing for interactions with your PBA can help you anticipate responses, refine your thoughts, and articulate your ideas better. This practice enhances your ability to communicate effectively and handle discussions with poise and confidence. You may practice this with colleagues, friends, family, or even your Buddy on your board.

Remember, the onus of personal development and improvement ultimately rests on your shoulders. By dedicating yourself to continuous learning and growth, you ensure that you are fully equipped to make the most of your board interactions and better prepared to implement their valuable insights.

Action and Reflection

As we wrap up Chapter 20, envision a better version of yourself on the other side of acting on some of the reflection points below!

1. Reflect on a recent interaction with someone from your PBA. Were you clear in expressing your thoughts? Were there moments of miscommunication? How can you improve next time?

2. Think about the last piece of feedback you received. Did you implement it? If not, why? If you did, what were the results?

3. Choose an upcoming topic or concern you plan to discuss with your PBA. Roleplay the conversation with a friend or colleague. Note the areas where you felt confident and where you stumbled.

4. Identify one area where you're hesitant to seek feedback. Dive into why. Is it fear of critique or something deeper?

5. Choose one skill (communication, active listening, giving feedback, etc.) and commit to improving it over the next month. Track your progress and seek feedback on your improvement.

Space for your notes and reflection.

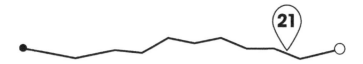

CHAPTER 21

ETHICAL CONSIDERATIONS AND BOARD DIVERSITY AND INCLUSION

"Diversity is not about how we differ. Diversity is about embracing one another's uniqueness."

Ola Joseph, a contemporary diversity and inclusion advocate

Reminder: DEIB stands for diversity, equity, inclusion, and belonging. This chapter focuses on the "D" and the "I" of this acronym.

In our rapidly globalizing world, the value of diversity and inclusivity within your PBA is undeniable. With a diverse board, you tap into a broader spectrum of experiences and insights, ensuring you're not confined by a limited or biased viewpoint. Without such diversity, you risk stagnation and, even worse, remain oblivious to blind spots that could hinder our progress. Yet to maintain effective diversity within your board, inclusion is paramount. Inclusivity elevates the board's dynamic by ensuring every member, regardless of their background, feels valued and heard. This inclusivity enriches your perspectives and reinforces the depth of your decisions.

But beyond diversity and inclusivity lies another pillar: ethics. It's not merely about doing what's right; it's about upholding the integrity of the advice you receive and the decisions you make. Ethical missteps might offer immediate gains, but the long-term consequences—damaged reputation, loss of trust, and potential professional setbacks—are far more significant and lasting.

By weaving together diversity, inclusion, and ethics, we not only strengthen the fabric of our PBA but also chart a path marked by growth, integrity, and a holistic understanding of the diverse world we navigate.

The Imperative of Ethics in Your PBA

"The measure of a person's character is what they would do if they knew they would never be found out."

Thomas B. Macaulay, British historian, essayist, and politician best known for his contributions to literature and his role in shaping British education policy

Navigating relationships with your PBA requires a strong ethical foundation. While these relationships are founded on trust and mutual respect, situations may arise that challenge your moral compass. Confidentiality, for instance, is paramount. Imagine a scenario where a board member shares sensitive information about industry trends in good faith, expecting discretion. Divulging this information, even unintentionally, could jeopardize their trust or even their professional standing.

Conflicts of interest are another potential pitfall. Suppose you have two advisors from competing firms or industries. Sharing insights from one with the other, even innocuously, could lead to accusations of favoritism or even corporate espionage. It's essential to be transparent about potential overlaps and to establish clear boundaries from the outset.

Integrity, however, goes beyond mere confidentiality and conflict avoidance. It's about being genuine in seeking advice, giving credit where it's due, and ensuring that the relationship is not exploitative.

Ask yourself: What are your core values, and do they resonate across your board? While each board member might bring a unique perspective, there should be a consistent ethical thread binding the relationships. Your non-negotiables, those principles you won't compromise on, need to be communicated and upheld. For instance, if honesty and transparency are your pillars, ensure that these are maintained in every interaction.

In your PBA journey, let your actions and decisions be consistently guided by a strong moral compass. Ensure that every interaction upholds the highest ethical standards, fostering an environment of trust, respect, and mutual growth.

True Diversity and Genuine Inclusion

Embracing diversity and inclusion in your PBA is more than just ticking boxes; it's about harnessing the power of varied perspectives to create a holistic and comprehensive career map. But how do we move beyond the buzzwords to genuinely integrate these values?

Firstly, let's understand the significance. A diverse board offers a mosaic of experiences, insights, and worldviews. This richness is invaluable, especially when navigating complex professional terrains. It's the difference between seeing the world through a single lens versus a kaleidoscope. However, diversity alone isn't enough. As American attorney, author, and workplace diversity advocate Vern Myers so aptly stated, "Diversity is being invited to the party; inclusion is being asked to dance." It's one thing to have diverse members on your board, but it's another to create an environment where every voice is not only heard but is also genuinely valued.

So, how do you "ask a board member to dance," metaphorically speaking? It begins with fostering an environment of respect and active listening. When a member shares an experience or perspective, give them your undivided attention. Ask questions. Be genuinely curious. And when opinions diverge, see the disagreement as an opportunity for growth, not confrontation.

Cultural sensitivity and awareness are at the heart of an inclusive board. This means recognizing that every individual's journey is shaped by a unique blend of cultural, societal, and personal experiences. It's about understanding these nuances and valuing them. Start by educating yourself on the backgrounds and cultures of your board members. Read, attend workshops, and even engage in open conversations with them about their experiences. This not only broadens your horizons but also signals to your board members that their backgrounds are acknowledged and respected.

Yet, even with the best intentions, biases, both conscious and unconscious, can creep in. Recognizing and challenging these biases is pivotal. For instance, if you find yourself always turning to a particular member for advice on a specific topic, ask yourself why. Is it because of their expertise, or is it a bias based on their background or gender? Regularly challenging such biases helps you derive the maximum value from your PBA, ensuring all members' insights are tapped into equitably.

The quest for an ethical, inclusive, and diverse PBA isn't a sprint; it's a marathon. It demands ongoing dedication, self-reflection, and an unwavering commitment to continuous learning. It's essential to remember that creating an inclusive and diverse PBA isn't about ticking boxes but genuinely fostering an environment that respects and values every individual's unique insight and experience. By anchoring your PBA in principles of cultural sensitivity, diversity, and ethics, you're not only enhancing the board's effectiveness but also creating a rich tapestry of experiences that propel collective growth.

Action and Reflection

Let's not just talk about ethics, diversity, and inclusion—let's take action!

1. Assess your PBA's current diversity. Are there perspectives, identity groups, or backgrounds that are missing?

2. Engage in open conversations with your board members about their experiences, fostering a culture of inclusion and understanding.

3. Regularly evaluate the ethical considerations guiding your PBA interactions. Are there areas of potential conflict or concern?

4. Challenge your biases. Reflect on the last few decisions or pieces of advice you sought from your PBA. Were they influenced by any biases?

5. Set aside time for self-reflection. Contemplate how you can ensure that your PBA remains rooted in ethics, diversity, and inclusivity.

Space for your notes and reflection.

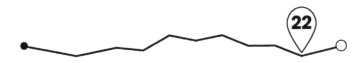

BOARD MEETINGS

*"Success is not about the destination,
but the journey along the way."*

*Zig Ziglar, an influential American author and motivational
speaker renowned for his inspirational talks and books
that have inspired countless individuals to achieve their
personal and professional goals*

Cultivating a diverse PBA encompassing mentors, peers, and mentees, is essential for comprehensive personal and professional growth. These advisors, with their unique perspectives, can become the cornerstone of your success, especially when navigating significant changes or addressing critical challenges in your professional journey. During such pivotal moments, bringing your board together "in one place" can not only accelerate ideation but also facilitate a collaborative environment where members build on each other's insights in unison. However, considering that your board may be dispersed geographically and members often have numerous commitments already, it's crucial to thoughtfully determine the necessity and logistics of a full board gathering. This chapter walks through how to plan, prepare, track, and harness the collective wisdom when such meetings are deemed beneficial.

Board Meetings | 213

Assessing the Need for a Full Board Meeting

When deciding whether to convene a full meeting of your PBA, it's essential to weigh several factors. Start by mapping out the primary issues you wish to address. If you're standing at a significant crossroads in your career, facing a monumental challenge, or grappling with a situation that demands varied expertise, a collective meeting of minds may be essential. For example, when I was launching a tech startup and my board comprised a tech veteran, a marketing guru, a financial whiz, and an HR specialist, bringing them together provided me with a holistic strategy that covered everything from product development to hiring practices. In contrast, if I were only facing a marketing challenge, perhaps a session with only the marketing expert would be necessary.

Next, consider the urgency of the issue. Routine updates and nonurgent matters can often be communicated individually, without the need to gather everyone. However, if the need is urgent and multifaceted, a full meeting may be warranted.

Once you've determined that your issue may merit a full board meeting, list the board members whose expertise aligns most directly with these challenges. If you find that a majority of your board's expertise areas are tapped into, it's an indicator that a collective session might be advantageous. If you choose to do a smaller board meeting, you might break into two groups based on the degree to which your advisors' areas of expertise intersect or diverge. If their domains are closely interrelated, their collective brainstorming may provide a multifaceted solution to a problem. Conversely, if other board members' areas of expertise are more disparate, it might indicate that your challenge spans multiple sectors or functions, and the collective wisdom of your entire board will be invaluable.

Requesting Participation

Once you've decided on a meeting, approach each board member with respect for their time and clear communication of your needs. Perhaps it's a dinner meeting if the board (or at least a large portion of it) is in the same geographic region. Could you cook for them? Take them out for dinner? It may be costly, but you aren't paying anyone besides perhaps the Coach, so this is a nice gesture. Who knows, maybe your Champion will pick up the bill. (And maybe you will pick up the bill when you become a Champion on someone else's board!) Alternatively, a virtual video call may be less of a burden if timing and coordination for an in-person meeting become difficult. Don't let perfection be the enemy of progress—bringing some board members together is better than none!

A sample email requesting that a board member attend a full PBA meeting might look like this:

> Dear [Advisor Name],
>
> I hope this message finds you well. I am planning a meeting of my Personal Board of Advisors to discuss some significant career developments and would greatly value your insights. The meeting will take place via video conference and is scheduled to last for one hour. Please let me know if you can attend. Your expertise is integral to this discussion.
>
> Please share which of the following days/times you are available:
> Option 1—Month, Date, one-hour time slot (time zone)
> Option 2—Month, Date, one-hour time slot (time zone)
> Option 3—Month, Date, one-hour time slot (time zone)
>
> Best,
> [Your Name]

I have used the tech tool Doodle to find time slots that work; in this case, recipients of the email can simply click a link and fill in their availability online. (There are other tech tools available for scheduling purposes as well.)

Head over to the companion website for more email templates such as this one and meeting agendas like the example below!

Proposed Meeting Agenda

When you've determined that a full board meeting is essential, effective planning and execution of the meeting are paramount. Before diving into the details of the meeting, be sure to set the stage. Sending out an agenda ahead of time not only demonstrates respect for your board members' time but also allows them to prepare, ensuring a more productive discussion. The agenda should be concise, focused, and tailored to your specific needs. While I'm providing a sample agenda below, remember to adapt it based on the unique purpose and objectives of your meeting. (Note that I'm suggesting you take the full hour for this full board meeting, not just fifty minutes as I've suggested in some of the previous chapters.)

- Introductions (10 minutes): Given that the board is diverse and members may not know each other, dedicate the first few minutes to introductions. This helps to establish a level of comfort and understanding among the participants.

- Review of Latest Career Developments (15 minutes): Share an update of your latest professional happenings, your accomplishments, changes in your career path, and lessons learned. This provides a comprehensive picture of your current state and prompts relevant discussions.

- Presentation of Career Map (15 minutes): Discuss your future plans, your intended career trajectory, and the steps you plan to take to achieve these goals. This gives your advisors a sense of your direction and allows them to provide targeted advice.

- Discussion of a Specific Challenge (10 minutes): Present a particular issue or question you're grappling with. Encourage open discussion and suggestions from the board members. This targeted dialogue can lead to creative solutions and strategies.

- Q&A and Closing (10 minutes): Allow for a Q&A session where board members can ask questions or provide further advice. Finish the meeting by thanking everyone for their time and valuable contributions. If possible, end early as a sign of respect for their time.

It's essential to note that the agenda provided is a guideline. Depending on your unique challenges and the expertise and familiarity of your board members, some sections might demand more time while others might be condensed or even omitted. The goal is to ensure a productive, respectful, and engaging session, fostering collective growth and meaningful insights.

Following the meeting, a gesture of appreciation such as a thank-you note goes a long way. It not only acknowledges their valuable contributions but also paves the way for future productive interactions.

Would it make sense to introduce some of your board members to each other so they can help fill out each other's boards? I've done this a few times because I thought it would help them, and in other circumstances, because I believed they needed some development themselves to better guide and support me.

Action and Reflection

We are in the home stretch, is it time to call your board to order yet now that Chapter 22 is done?

1. Reflect on the current challenges or decisions you're facing in your professional journey. Which of these would benefit from the collective insights of your PBA? Are there specific challenges that can be addressed by one or two specific board members rather than the entire board?

2. List each board member and their primary area of expertise. Are there overlapping domains or unique areas that you haven't tapped into recently? How might the combined insights of these experts benefit your current situation?

3. Consider your board members' preferences. Would they appreciate a formal invitation, an informal chat, or perhaps a tool like Doodle for scheduling? Reflect on the tone and content of your communications. How can you ensure clarity while expressing genuine respect and gratitude for their time?

4. Tailor the sample agenda to fit your current needs. Which items are most crucial for your upcoming meeting? Are there items that can be shortened, extended, or omitted entirely? Reflect on past meetings (if any). Were there segments that felt rushed or parts that could have been more concise?

5. Reflect on the dynamics between board members during the meeting. Were there synergies that could be further explored? Consider introducing board members who might benefit from knowing each other. What mutual benefits could arise from such introductions?

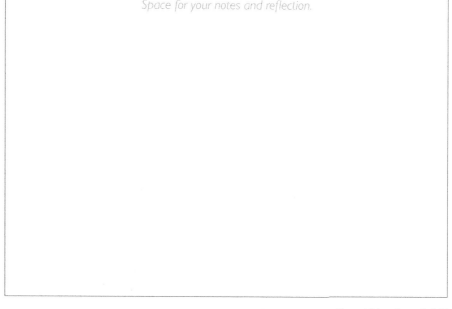

Space for your notes and reflection.

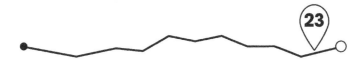

CHAPTER 23

MEASURING AND EVALUATING BOARD EFFECTIVENESS

"If you can't measure it, you can't improve it."

Peter Drucker, a pioneering Austrian-American management consultant and author whose groundbreaking work laid the foundation for modern management theory and practice

The journey of developing your PBA and charting your career map is one of continuous evolution. To facilitate growth, it's crucial to gauge the effectiveness of your board interactions and the impact of their contributions. In this chapter, we will build out a systematic approach to tracking progress and evaluating impact to allow for adaptive changes and continuous improvement in your journey.

Establishing Metrics

Metrics serve as quantifiable indicators of progress; the key lies in understanding their significance and adapting based on their insights. Let's consider one particular metric: the number of strategic conversations.

You need to begin by defining the metric you're measuring and setting a target.

Defining "Strategic Conversations"

At its core, a strategic conversation isn't just any discussion; it's a dialogue that brings forth valuable insights, challenges existing perspectives and helps shape future actions. It's a conversation that aligns with and potentially advances your professional goals.

Setting a Target

How do you decide on a "good" number of strategic conversations? Begin by setting a realistic target based on your current status and your goals. If you're in a phase where you're actively seeking guidance, perhaps aim for one strategic conversation per week. If you're in a more reflective phase, one per month might be appropriate.

Now let's talk about interpreting the metrics:

Not Meeting the Target

Implication: If you're not achieving your target number of strategic conversations, it might indicate that you're not actively seeking enough input or setting aside dedicated time for such dialogues.

Action: Reevaluate your commitments and priorities. Schedule regular sessions with board members or industry peers. Consider attending relevant seminars or webinars where strategic discussions are likely.

Meeting the Target

Implication: You're on track! The conversations you're having align with your goal.

Action: Continue with your current approach, and always ensure the quality of these conversations remains high. The ultimate goal won't be reached purely through quantity but through the value derived from each dialogue.

Overshooting the Target

Implication: Engaging in more strategic conversations than you targeted might suggest you're in an intense phase of learning or decision making. However, it could also mean you're stretching yourself thin or not filtering the quality of your engagements.

Action: Reflect on the nature of these extra conversations. Are they genuinely strategic, or are some of them routine check-ins? Prioritize quality over quantity. If you're feeling overwhelmed, consider spacing out these discussions to allow time for reflection and implementation of insights.

In the early phase of my startup journey, I set a target to have at least three strategic conversations per month. After three months, I noticed I was averaging five. On reflection, while the additional conversations provided diverse insights, I felt I wasn't dedicating enough time to act on the advice I was receiving. I decided to maintain my initial target and became more selective, ensuring each conversation was truly strategic. This allowed me to balance input with action, making the most of the insights I garnered.

Other Metrics to Guide Your PBA Journey

As you have gathered by now, my analytical mind and engineering education(s) drive me toward process, structure, and data. This section discusses a few metrics that you may want to incorporate into your PBA process: what to measure, how to calculate, and actions to take when things get "out of whack."

Feedback Implementation Rate

Description: Track the percentage of actionable feedback from your PBA that you've implemented. This metric helps gauge how effectively you're putting the advice into practice.

Corrective Action: If your rate is low, reflect on potential barriers preventing implementation. Are the suggestions not aligning with your goals, or are there other challenges?

Advisor Engagement Frequency

Description: Measure how often you engage with each board member. This helps ensure that you're not overly reliant on one advisor and that you're tapping into the diverse expertise of your board.

Corrective Action: If there's an imbalance, consider scheduling more frequent check-ins with less engaged advisors. Their unique perspectives might offer fresh insights.

Diversity Quotient

Description: Assess the diversity of your board in terms of industry background, demographics, experience levels, etc. A diverse board can offer a broader range of insights.

Corrective Action: If you find your board lacks diversity in any aspect, consider seeking new members to fill these gaps.

Personal Growth Index

Description: Assess your growth over time, considering factors like skill development, expanded networks, confidence in decision making, etc. Consider these in relation to when you began engaging with your PBA and/or the last time your PBA was refreshed.

Corrective Action: If you feel as though you are stagnating, it might be time to seek new challenges or request specific guidance from your PBA on areas you wish to improve.

Board Rotation Rate

Description: Monitor how frequently new advisors join your board and how often others depart. This can indicate the dynamism and freshness of your PBA.

Corrective Action: If there's a high rotation rate, ensure it's for growth reasons and not because advisors feel undervalued. Conversely, if there's little to no rotation, ponder if fresh perspectives could benefit you.

Advisor Satisfaction Score

Description: Periodically survey your advisors on their experience in your PBA. Are they satisfied with the engagement? Do they feel their insights are valued and implemented?

Corrective Action: Low scores might necessitate a discussion about improving the PBA dynamics, ensuring every member feels respected and engaged.

Each of these metrics serves as a compass helping you navigate your PBA journey more effectively. While metrics provide valuable insights, remember to balance data-driven decisions with intuition and personal judgment. The key is to use these metrics as tools to enhance, not dictate, your interactions and growth.

The companion website shares more information on these metrics along with others that you may include in your PBA process as well as resources to make the calculations a bit easier when tracking over time.

Engaging in Self-Reflection

A crucial component of evaluation is self-reflection. Regular introspection enables you to consider the effectiveness of your strategies and the impact of your PBA. Ask yourself the critical start-stop-continue-shift questions:

- What should I start doing?
- What should I stop doing?
- What practices should I modify?
- What's working well and should continue?

-iring Process, Steps 4–8

We're picking the -iring process back up from Part I. Previously we covered the ways to Desire, Inquire, and Hire.

Admire (Thank You!)

Thank your board members and share your appreciation of the progress that you've made with their help. You can do this as frequently as you find natural. It's never a bad time to express admiration and say thanks!

Upon accepting my first full-time job offer, my first call after my family was to a mentor from my high school days to thank him for his guidance. His advice was "Pete, no matter how successful you become or what title you have or how much money you make, remember that the success of a man is based on the relationships he has with his God, his family, and his friends—in that order." Clearly, this stuck with me more than a decade later, Rich.

Fire

The distinction between "retiring" and "firing" someone from your PBA lies in the immediacy and nature of the action. While "firing" implies a direct, immediate response to a significant event or action, "retiring" indicates a more gradual realization that the alignment between you and a board member has diminished over time.

There are instances where it becomes evident that a board member is no longer a suitable fit. This could be due to a noticeable lack of commitment or a consistent failure to meet previously agreed-upon expectations. Navigating such a situation requires sensitivity and tact, particularly when it comes to having that potentially challenging conversation about ending the relationship. It's crucial to approach this discussion with a clear mind, focus on facts, and try your best to keep emotional reactions in check.

If you've been diligently reviewing and reassessing your goals and expectations with the board member you need to fire, the decision to part ways is unlikely to come as a shock to either party. Preparation is essential. Before the conversation, reflect on the reasons for this decision and anticipate potential responses. During the discussion, be straightforward, honest, and appreciative of their contributions. Afterward, it's good practice to send a follow-up email documenting the conversation. This written record provides clarity and ensures both parties are on the same page. Most importantly, despite the decision to part ways, always express gratitude for the time and insights the board member shared with you.

Retire

Retiring a board member is a subtler form of parting ways compared to the directness of firing them. In such cases, there's no negative event or action that triggers the decision. Instead, it's often a realization that your needs have evolved, your priorities have shifted or realigned, or you've collectively achieved the goals you initially set out to accomplish. When broaching the process of retirement, it's imperative to start by expressing sincere gratitude for the board members' contributions. Their guidance and insights have been extremely valuable, and expressing this is crucial. Following this acknowledgment, communicate your decision with respect and clarity. It's essential to convey that this decision stems from your evolving professional landscape and not from any shortcomings on their part. If applicable, discuss the transition of their responsibilities to new board members who are more aligned with your current career objectives. This ensures continuity and sets the stage for the next phase of your professional journey.

As you go through life, your priorities can and likely will shift—this is okay. There will probably be phases of work-work-work, and there will also be phases of live-live-live.

Over time, it's ideal to find a true, sustainable, and manageable balance between the two. Work–life balance and work–life integration aren't one-size-fits-all. Retiring certain board members will likely occur as you navigate various phases of your journey.

Rewire

Refreshing or "rewiring" your board is a proactive approach to ensuring its continued relevance and effectiveness as you progress in your career. Start by identifying areas where you feel a fresh perspective could be beneficial. This could mean seeking out potential new board members who offer unique expertise and insights that you currently lack. The goal is to find individuals who can challenge your existing paradigms and open doors to new growth opportunities. As you evaluate your board, consider your evolving professional needs and any skill gaps that might have emerged. By regularly assessing these aspects and making necessary adjustments, you ensure that your board remains attuned to your journey, providing invaluable guidance every step of the way.

In Chapter 5 we talked about your ikigai (passion, mission, profession, and vocation), and as we reflect on opportunities to "rewire" our boards, we can ask ourselves a few other questions. Tim taught me about the entrepreneurial operating system (EOS) as I was building my company, and he helped me with a few of the concepts in this book as well. Tim pointed me to Gino Wickman's book *The EOS Life* which asks the following questions (which we could and probably should be asking ourselves every three to six months). Are you . . .

1. **Doing what you love?**
2. **With people you love?**
3. **Making a huge difference?**
4. **Being compensated appropriately?**
5. **With time for other passions?**

Inspire

As you continue to grow and evolve in your career, it's worth considering how you can pay it forward. One meaningful way to do this is by joining someone else's board and taking on the role of a mentor or a successor. This not only allows you to impart the wisdom and insights you've gained but also enriches your own understanding from a mentor's perspective. Engaging in such roles reinforces the symbiotic nature of professional relationships. To find opportunities where you can offer your expertise, consider reaching out to your current board members and work peers—they might be aware of individuals within their networks who are seeking valuable contributors for their boards. Starting with one or two such positions can be a fulfilling way to give back while also expanding your own professional horizons.

"The unexamined life is not worth living."

Socrates, a witty ancient Greek who stirred up Athens with
his relentless questioning and turned philosophy into a lively,
never-ending quest for wisdom and truth

Expanding to Specialized Roles as Needed

As your professional journey unfolds, there will be times when specialized guidance becomes essential. The basic structure of your PBA can and should evolve based on your current needs and aspirations. While the core members of your board provide holistic advice, certain challenges or growth phases might necessitate specific expertise. These are a few specialized board seats to consider adding to your board:

Well-Being Advisor: Whether they're a therapist or a clinical psychologist, this individual aids in stress management, emotional resilience, and cognitive reprogramming. They help you address mental health concerns, alter negative thought patterns, and proactively manage your well-being.

Physical Wellness Guide: Your fitness coach assists in curating exercise regimens, fostering healthy habits, and ensuring a balanced lifestyle conducive to peak professional performance.

Personal Growth Mentor: A life coach emphasizes aligning your personal aspirations with your professional goals. They guide you in self-reflection, goal setting, and living a life congruent with your values.

Career Development Expert: An executive coach zeroes in on strategic planning, career transitions, skill enhancement, and workplace accountability. They offer motivation, confidence-boosting, and high-level career development strategies.

Naysayer: Ideally, this role is built into your core board members, but I wanted to highlight this aspect of a board member here. They play "devil's advocate" by always questioning and challenging your ideas. They compel you to consider alternative viewpoints and potential pitfalls.

Fly-By Mentor: This is not a permanent seat-holder but someone you consult sporadically for specific insights or fresh perspectives.

Bench Members: These are potential future board members or specialists you keep in touch with. While they might not have a formal role at the moment, maintaining a warm relationship ensures they are available when their expertise becomes relevant.

It's worth noting that while having a therapist is becoming a normalized aspect of professional life, it's not just for crisis moments. Being proactive in seeking emotional and mental support can equip you with tools and strategies before challenges arise.

Remember, seeking guidance, whether for career challenges or personal well-being, is a strength, not a weakness. It's OK to confide in professionals, and sometimes it's even more beneficial than relying solely on friends and family. Your PBA is there to ensure every facet of your life aligns with your overarching vision and goals, and this includes your mental and emotional well-being.

In the book **Healing: Our Path from Mental Illness to Mental Health** *by Thomas Insel, MD, Insel shares a story regarding a treatment for anxiety and depression called the "Friendship Bench." This method of a, multiperson "listening ear" support system on public park benches was used in Zimbabwe when it was recognized that social connection with an empathic, trusted older adult could be a powerful intervention for those struggling with mental health issues.*

I took a break from writing this chapter to attend a speech by retired Army Command Sergeant Major Gretchen Evans. Multiple peers and mentors had suggested I hear her speak, and I am very glad that I heeded their guidance—this was one of the most inspiring one-hour speaking sessions I have ever witnessed in person. Evans shared how she fought to find a life of meaning and one worth living when she found her "rope team" who, like members of a rock-climbing team (or your PBA), commit to standing firm and holding you up when you need it most. "If someone slips, the rest of us pick you up," she explained. "There's safety and accountability in that. You have to be connected to other people in your life who are committed to you."[28]

Communicating (and Celebrating) Success

One critical aspect of your journey with your PBA is acknowledging and celebrating your progress. Whether you've achieved a milestone on your career map, met or surpassed the "board success metrics" you've set, or overcome other challenges, each accomplishment deserves recognition. But it's not just about patting yourself on the back; it's also about sharing these successes with your PBA, the group of individuals who have been instrumental in guiding and advising you. Sharing your success with them allows them to see the tangible impact of their contributions and reinforces the value they bring to your professional journey.

---

28 Evans, G. 2018. *Leading from the Front.* CreateSpace Independent Publishing Platform.

Career Map Progress: As you move along your predefined career map, there will be specific checkpoints or goals. When you reach these, take a moment to reflect and share this progress with your board. "I've successfully transitioned into the new role we discussed, and the insights you provided on organizational dynamics were spot-on" is one quick and easy message to share.

Metrics-Based Achievements: If you've set specific "board success metrics" such as having a particular number of strategic conversations per month or reaching a certain professional development target, achieving these metrics is a clear indicator of progress. Celebrate these moments by sharing your results with your board. For example, you could say, "Thanks to our strategic discussions last month, I was able to lead my team to exceed our quarterly targets. Your insights were invaluable."

Overcoming Challenges: Not all progress is about reaching positive milestones. Sometimes, the way you navigate challenges or setbacks, with the guidance of your PBA is, in itself, an achievement. Share these stories too, with messages like "The strategy we brainstormed to address the team conflict worked wonders. We're now more cohesive than ever."

Beyond just sharing the good news, consider ways to involve your board in a celebration. Whether it's a simple thank-you note, a shared meal (virtual or in-person), or even a group call to express gratitude, these gestures go a long way. They not only acknowledge the board's role in your successes but also foster a deeper bond, ensuring continued collaboration and mutual growth.

Mentors are typically busy individuals unless they are retired (and even then they are likely busy playing pickleball, traveling, consulting, or volunteering). Appreciating their time and making the most of the moments they share with you will not only make you a more considerate mentee but also a more effective learner.

Here is a thank-you note template suggestion. If possible, I recommend you write it out by hand!

[Their Name],

Thank you for taking the time to discuss X on Y date. This was valuable for me on [1-2-3] fronts, and as a result, I am now doing A (or I now understand B). I will continue to work on C and shall share my progress with you leading up to our next conversation on D date.

[My Name]

The companion website also holds a few clever ways to incorporate digital media into the PBA and career mapping process. Social shoutouts are easy when you have a template to copy and paste at your fingertips.

Another way to celebrate is to offer thanks publicly. Ask relevant board members if it would be OK to highlight your work together on a LinkedIn post. Bonus points if you have a selfie together to post or a snapshot from your video call.

Here's an example of a thank-you you could post to LinkedIn:

> *Special thanks to my functional mentor @NAME for taking the time to meet with me this week. It's been very helpful growing together over the last three months together. My aha moment from our most recent session was X, and I look forward to implementing Y as a result. #mentorship #PersonalBoardOfAdvisors #GiveLattitude*

Action and Reflection

As we wrap up Chapter 23, start to think about what you are tracking today and which part of the "-iring" process you are in at this stage of the book. Let's put it to the test.

You may have other board seats that are not listed above. If so, please share your thoughts at: Pathfinders@GoLattitude.com (or on the companion website).

1. When did you last review your ikigai progress and could you add some reminders to your calendar to review the other five questions from *The EOS Life*?

2. Is there a board member who is no longer following the agreed-upon goals and expectations? Are they canceling or rescheduling multiple meetings in a row or failing to follow through on action items after you followed up?

3. Just as Peter Drucker said, "If you can't measure it, you can't improve it." Regularly measure the effectiveness of your board interactions and the impact of their guidance. Consider setting up a quarterly review to evaluate your board's contributions to your goals and milestones.

4. Clearly define what metrics you will use to gauge the effectiveness of your PBA. Whether it's the number of strategic conversations, advisor engagement frequency, or feedback implementation rate, knowing these figures will guide your next steps.

5. Continuously reassess the alignment of your board members with your evolving needs. Remember, it's OK to "fire" or "retire" members if they no longer fit. Conversely, it may be time to "rewire" your board by adding members who offer fresh perspectives or fill current gaps.

6. Remember to celebrate your achievements, big or small. Share these milestones with your board members, as they've been instrumental in your journey. Whether it's through a simple thank-you note, a shared meal, or a LinkedIn shout-out, show appreciation. Try using a #PersonalBoardOfAdvisors or #PBAwins in your post on social media.

7. Routinely evaluate your own performance and growth. Ask yourself the critical start-stop-continue-shift questions to understand what's working and what's not. Take ownership of your growth, seeking guidance where needed.

8. As you gain experience and knowledge, consider how you can be of value to others. Offer to join someone else's board, serve as a mentor, or simply share the wisdom you've acquired. Remember: the cycle of learning and giving back enriches not only your professional journey but also the broader community in which you live, play, and work.

Space for your notes and reflection.

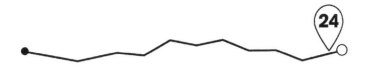

CHAPTER 24

LEVERAGING RESOURCES, TECHNOLOGY, AND DIGITAL TOOLS

"Technology is just a tool. In terms of getting the kids working together and motivating them, the teacher is the most important."

Bill Gates, a guy who's pretty good at building companies and knows a lot about computers

In the age of digitization, we find ourselves amidst a plethora of resources designed to enhance our productivity, streamline processes, and improve communication. As we venture forth in this chapter and seek to build and manage our PBA, technology will play an invaluable role, offering innovative tools for effective board management and career development.

Over the last few years, I developed a tool to grow with you as you progress through this book; hopefully, you'll be using it soon! However, there are several other tools worth considering for their utility in managing your board and career development. As you assess each one, remember to decide whether you'd rather "make" it (spending time/resources) or "buy" it (spending money).

Assessing Your Technological Landscape

To harness technology effectively, it's crucial to start by assessing the tools and platforms you're currently using. Examine how you use technology in both your personal and professional lives. Then, identify if there are components of managing your PBA that could benefit from automation or enhanced efficiency. This involves delving into every aspect, from the way you communicate with board members to how you manage tasks, execute projects, and store data. The goal is to optimize and streamline using the technological resources you already have at your disposal.

Researching Relevant Tools

Once you've identified potential areas for enhancement, delve into researching digital solutions tailored to these needs. With the increasing prevalence of apps and platforms designed for mentorship, project management, communication, and collaboration, finding a tool that resonates with your needs is more achievable than ever. Be mindful of the tool's usability, compatibility with your existing systems, and its ability to grow with you as your PBA expands and evolves.

Creating a Technology Plan

With your research at hand, devise a technology plan. This roadmap should detail the tools you intend to adopt, what they cost, their features, and your timeline for their integration. This plan serves as a blueprint for digital transformation, guiding you toward more efficient PBA management.

Seeking Training and Support

The adoption of new technology often comes with a learning curve. Ensure you're maximizing your chosen tools' potential by seeking adequate training or support. This investment in skill development can range from attending workshops and webinars to exploring online tutorials. Learning how to proficiently use your selected tools can greatly enhance their effectiveness in your PBA management.

Regularly Evaluate and Update

As you navigate your digital journey, you need to continually assess your chosen technology's effectiveness. Is the tool enhancing your productivity? Has communication improved? Be open to adjusting or exploring new tools to keep abreast with the ever-evolving digital landscape and your shifting needs.

"Technology is best when it brings people together."

Matt Mullenweg, an entrepreneur and computer programmer best known as the cofounder of WordPress, one of the most widely used content management systems (CMS) for websites and blogs

Your Personal Board Toolkit

Having the right tools can profoundly enhance the management of your PBA. Your toolkit should be a blend of digital resources, practical templates, and reflective exercises to help you navigate, monitor, and optimize your PBA interactions. Here's a detailed breakdown of what could go into your "starter" personal board toolkit.

Companion Website: This website, designed specifically for readers of this book, offers a comprehensive platform to set up and manage your career map and PBA. It comes with built-in worksheets, reference documents, and interactive features for seamless board management (and it will keep improving over time). Ideally, you'll check this out before exploring the other options, but my job is to arm you with choices!

External Scheduling Tools: Digital calendars or scheduling apps that allow you to coordinate meetings with your board members effortlessly, ensuring you never miss a strategic conversation.

External Document-Sharing Platforms: Tools like Google Drive, Dropbox, or OneDrive enable real-time collaboration and document sharing, which are vital for sharing agendas, notes, or reference materials.

The following resources can be found on the companion website, go check them out and start using them!

Goal Setting and Progress-Tracking Templates

- **Career Map Blueprint:** Use this to chart out your career trajectory, identifying key milestones, potential challenges, and strategies.
- **PBA Meeting Agenda Template:** A standardized template ensures your meetings are structured, focused, and productive.

Reflection Exercises

- **Feedback Loop Workbook:** Regularly capture feedback from your board members and use this workbook to analyze, reflect upon, and act on the insights provided.
- **Self-Assessment Sheets:** Periodically assess your growth, challenges, and changing needs to ensure your PBA remains aligned with your evolving goals.

Infographics and Visual Aids

- **Essential Elements of the Personal Board Toolkit:** This quick visual guide summarizes all the tools you have collected and how to use them effectively.

- **PBA Interaction Flowchart:** This illustrative guide shows how to navigate through different stages of PBA interactions, from onboarding to feedback and goal setting.

While technology and tools can offer support, the real power lies in how you use them. Regularly update your toolkit, adapting to new challenges and opportunities. Remember, the ultimate goal is to streamline your interactions, making the PBA experience enriching and transformative for your career journey.

Educational Sessions and Workshops

If you're feeling overwhelmed by the idea of building or managing your PBA, consider attending one of my workshops. These offer hands-on experience, expert insights, and networking opportunities with fellow professionals on a similar journey. Reach out on the companion website or send an email to Pathfinders@GoLattitude.com.

Action and Reflection

As we wrap up Chapter 24, start to think about what you can be doing today and what you may already be doing but just not tracking ... yet!

1. Conduct a comprehensive review of your current digital tools and platforms. List what you're using and identify any redundancies or gaps. This will help you understand which tools can be eliminated, which need to be added, and where you can integrate for more efficiency.

2. Set aside time to download, explore, and familiarize yourself with this book's companion website. This tool is tailored to the PBA process, and fully leveraging it can greatly simplify board management.

3. Create or download the suggested templates, such as the Career Map Blueprint and PBA Meeting Agenda Template. Begin populating them to track progress and ensure structured board meetings.

4. If you're integrating a new tool or platform, sign up for an online tutorial, webinar, or workshop to ensure you're maximizing its features.

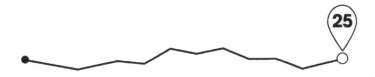

CHAPTER 25:

EXPLORING ORGANIZATIONAL USE CASES

"The only way to do great work is to love what you do."

Steve Jobs, we can thank him for the iPhone and many other pieces of technology that ping us daily and help us get work done

In today's volatile job market, employee loyalty isn't just about competitive salaries or appealing perks. It's about belonging, professional growth, and feeling genuinely valued. The PBA methodology, when integrated within an organizational framework, can be a catalyst for creating such an environment.

This chapter shifts from addressing individual readers who would be using the career map/ PBA personally, to focusing on readers who might consider helping their organization integrate this methodology as a high-level value-add.

Employee-focused companies that succeed in the future need to demonstrate a commitment and loyalty to their employees by giving them something that they can use for the rest of their lives—the groundwork to develop their own PBA. The return on investment (ROI) is evident: when employees put the PBA concepts into practice and engage, they will feel a stronger sense of belonging, have a clear map to professional growth, and are empowered. Over time turnover will drop and productivity will increase. Lower turnover then reduces recruitment costs while enhancing organizational culture, making the company more attractive to prospective talent. With structured PBA engagement like this, the organization is likely to see other benefits such as improved performance, shorter learning cycles, faster work completion, and greater collaboration, while creating and sustaining a place where the employee feels valued and to which they therefore remain committed.

Operationalizing PBA in Organizations

We can all agree that people being connected at work is a great idea and that over time, the company will be more profitable. Now let's talk about how to actually put these ideas into action at work for our teams.

Onboarding and Integration Process

The onboarding period is a crucial phase for a new employee. It's during this time that they familiarize themselves with the organization's culture, vision, and their role within it. Introducing the idea of a PBA and encouraging them to build their board with mentors from within the organization can help them integrate more seamlessly, gain support, and feel a sense of belonging. Similarly, presenting them with the concept of career maps can help them visualize their potential growth within the organization, creating a more concrete sense of purpose and direction.

Professional and Career Development

The PBA serves as a powerful tool for ongoing professional and career development. As employees progress in their careers, their advisors can provide insights, feedback, and guidance, helping them navigate challenges and make informed decisions. Career maps, meanwhile, offer a visual representation of their career journey, enabling them to identify necessary skills, experiences, and milestones they need to achieve to advance within the organization.

Retention Strategy for Top Talent

In a competitive landscape, retaining top talent is paramount. Offering employees the opportunity to establish a PBA and develop a career map demonstrates an organization's commitment to their growth and development. This proactive approach to talent development can significantly improve job satisfaction, engagement, and consequently retention.

Attracting Top Talent

Demonstrating that it invests in employees by helping them establish PBAs and develop career maps can make an organization more attractive to prospective talent. These initiatives suggest a nurturing and supportive work environment that places significant emphasis on employee growth and development.

Sharing Success Stories

Organizations can further enhance their talent development strategy by sharing success stories. Social media shout-outs or other ways of recognizing personal board members and the impact they've made can serve as powerful testimonials. These narratives can be shared internally to inspire other employees and externally to showcase the organization's commitment to its people. Podcasts and short video interviews are some other easy ways to put this concept into action!

Addressing Concerns of External Advisors

It's natural to wonder, "What if our employees fill board seats with external advisors?" Remember that external perspectives can offer fresh insights and broaden an employee's network, ultimately benefiting the organization. Nearly every workshop that I have conducted with high-level leaders and executives has reinforced that it is OK to have external guides on your PBA. Let's face it, if our people are going to leave because we are not giving enough guidance, restricting their professional development will likely only accelerate the departure.

Securing Leadership Buy-In for the PBA Initiative

To champion the integration of the PBA and career maps within your organization, it's imperative to articulate their value convincingly to leadership. When seeking support and potential funding, start by pinpointing the immediate and long-term benefits:

1. Emphasize how the PBA framework can refine decision-making, streamline collaborations, and amplify individual contributions to team objectives.

2. Demonstrate how nurturing individual growth through a PBA can directly bolster team performance and further the company's overarching mission. Furthermore, the PBA model, by design, fosters leadership skills, equipping employees for heightened organizational responsibilities.

3. Reinforce the tangible returns the organization stands to gain. By investing in the PBA methodology, the company can expect optimized outcomes, reduced turnover, and a culture that's driven by continuous learning and collaboration.

4. Highlight that companies known for investing in employee growth not only retain talent but become magnets for top-tier professionals in the industry.

Approach leadership with enthusiasm, armed with whatever data and case studies you can find to underscore the transformative potential of the PBA and career maps. Tailor the pitch to the company's unique challenges and goals, showing how this initiative can be a solution. And, if you encounter roadblocks, consider collaborating with HR or employee resource groups, as they often have insights into developmental strategies and might already be seeking innovative methods like the PBA framework.

The following template provides an example of an email to leadership recommending the adoption of the PBA/career map framework.

Subject: Proposal: Enhancing Employee Growth with the Personal Board of Advisors Framework

Dear [Leader's Name],

I hope this message finds you well. Over the past few months, as I've been deeply involved in our team's projects and growth initiatives, I've been reflecting on the core values and strategies we often discuss. Our conversations about professional development, mentorship, and fostering a culture of continuous learning resonate strongly with me.

Recently, I came across a compelling resource that aligns with our discussions and the direction we envision for our team. The book is titled **Pathfinders: Navigating Your Career Map with a Personal Board of Advisors.** It introduces a structured approach to professional growth. By actively integrating mentors and advisors (collectively called the Personal Board of Advisors, or PBA) into one's professional journey, this framework can significantly amplify individual contributions to team and organizational objectives.

Here's why I believe this could be transformational for us:

- By tapping into a diverse network of mentors, employees can refine decision-making and collaboration skills, leading to optimized outcomes for our projects.
- The PBA model fosters skills that directly bolster team performance, furthering our overarching mission.
- As we invest in our team's growth, we can expect reduced turnover and a heightened culture of learning and collaboration.
- Championing such initiatives will also better position us to attract the industry's best.
- I've been informally applying some of the book's principles, and the insights have been immensely valuable. Given our company's forward-thinking approach and our shared commitment to professional development, I believe a more formal integration of the PBA framework could be a game changer.

I'd love the opportunity to discuss this further, perhaps even exploring a pilot program or workshop based on the book's methodology. I genuinely believe that this can be the catalyst to drive our team to new heights.

Thank you for considering this proposal. I eagerly await your thoughts.

Warm regards,

[Your Name]

Expanding PBA Application Beyond Traditional Work Settings

The principles underlying the PBA and career maps extend far beyond conventional workplaces. Their adaptive nature makes them applicable in diverse settings, ranging from professional associations to educational institutions. In fact, anyone on the brink of a pivotal life transition would find value in them.

Associations and Member Engagement

Professional associations, often hubs for networking and collaboration, can greatly benefit from integrating the PBA model and career maps. Such an approach can catalyze deeper, more structured member engagement. By encouraging members to curate their advisory boards and craft their career trajectories, associations can offer a platform for making intentional connections and pooling collective wisdom and experiences. At your next membership meeting, propose the incorporation of PBAs. It might just be the catalyst your group needs to facilitate transformative, meaningful interactions.

Educational Institutions and Career Services

Introducing the PBA model and career maps within educational settings can be a game changer. Specifically, career services offices in colleges and universities can use these tools to offer students more than just job placement assistance. By guiding students to build their PBAs and map out their career paths, these offices can ensure that students not only find jobs but also embark on fulfilling, well-guided professional journeys. Such a structured approach can significantly enrich students' academic and preprofessional experiences, setting them up for long-term success.

Gifts for Life Transitions

The PBA model and career maps are invaluable tools for individuals facing significant crossroads in their lives. Consider this book and its accompanying website as thoughtful gifts for:

- **High School Graduates:** As these graduates stand on the threshold of higher education or the professional world, equipping them with these tools can offer clarity and direction.

- **College or University Graduates:** As these graduates transition from academia to the professional realm, a PBA can be their compass, ensuring they navigate the early stages of their careers with guidance and mentorship.

- **Individuals Pursuing Alternative Career Paths:** Not everyone pursues higher education. For those diving into trades, starting an entrepreneurial venture, or exploring another unconventional profession, the PBA model can serve as a structured guide, helping them carve out their unique paths.

Action and Reflection

That's the last chapter of the book before the conclusion. We've almost made it! Are you ready to make a big splash at work? Remember, you now have the companion website to get started in a "little to no tech" manner right now!

1. Consider the current talent management strategies in place within your organization. Are they aligned with the values and benefits of the PBA methodology? It may be time to conduct a survey or feedback session to gauge employee sentiment about mentorship, professional growth, and belonging within the company.

2. How might you test the PBA and career maps framework in a small department or team within your organization? One idea is to initiate a pilot program to introduce the PBA concept to a select group. Monitor its impact on engagement, collaboration, and job satisfaction to determine whether this program could benefit the entire organization and/or if any adjustments are necessary.

3. Who are the influential stakeholders within your organization that could champion the integration of the PBA methodology?

4. Think about your broader community—associations, educational institutions, etc. How could the PBA concept be introduced or amplified in these settings?

Space for your notes and reflection.

CONCLUSION:

YOUR PERSONAL BOARD OF ADVISORS JOURNEY

*"Life is what you make of it, and together
we can indeed change the world and move mountains.
Together almost anything is possible."*

Pete Schramm

How does your career map look now, and how many open board seats do you have? No matter your answers, you took the first step toward progress by reading this book. Now you have the tools, your map is in hand, and you're ready to find the proper guides for your journey. Let's do a quick refresher and then send you on your way!

In our exploration, we've underscored the significance of the career map, a visual testament to one's professional journey. This tool uniquely captures where you've been, where you are now, and where you see yourself in the future. Crucially, the "future" stages of your map should present a few viable options, embodying the fluidity and myriad possibilities of professional life. Structurally, the career map comprises five distinct columns that breathe life into each phase of your journey: the role or job you occupied, the skills you honed, the education and certifications you earned, the notable accomplishments you achieved, and the fun personal experiences that shaped you.

To truly optimize the power of your career map, integrating insights from your PBA is crucial. These mentors and guides not only offer a wealth of advice and perspectives but are instrumental in navigating the uncertainties and choices that the map will inevitably present. They can also assist in populating those columns, ensuring that the full spectrum of your professional experiences is richly detailed and aligned with your aspirations. Remember, as you progress and revisit and refine your map, the insights from your PBA will be invaluable in ensuring it remains a true reflection of your goals and the paths you're keen to explore.

With your career map in hand, you are better equipped to chart your professional growth, aided by the wisdom of your PBA. This map not only marks milestones but also serves as a dynamic blueprint for the future. Engage with it, iterate on it with your PBA, and let it guide you to a fulfilling professional journey filled with purpose, growth, and passion.

Board Seat Recap

Here are the ten prospective board seats to consider when building our PBA. Remember: eight is an ideal number, but you can start with as few as three or four and build from there! If you already have a board, periodically review these roles and consider whether your board needs a refresh to align with shifting priorities and professional goals.

Buddy: The Peer Support Advisor

Symbolized by the life jacket, our Buddy is our immediate support system in the turbulent waters of professional life. As we navigate the intricacies of our roles, this colleague or peer offers a stabilizing influence, providing companionship, sage advice, and an empathetic ear. Their essence lies not in steering our career trajectory but in offering consistent support that enhances our day-to-day work experience and fosters deeper engagement and satisfaction.

Accountability Partner: The Commitment Enforcer and Responsibility Advisor

Embodied by the steadfast anchor, our Accountability Partner ensures we remain grounded in our commitments. Rooted in mutual respect and shared objectives, this relationship stands out in its reciprocity. More than merely a mentor or Sponsor, this partnership emphasizes unwavering commitment and motivation, forging a bond that keeps us anchored in our goals.

Functional Mentor: The Experienced Guide and Inside Advisor

Represented by the compass, the Functional Mentor charts a course through the vast expanse of their experiences. They've journeyed through terrains we have yet to explore, making their insights invaluable. While they share their wisdom, they leave it to us to embark on our unique journey, ensuring we find our true north.

Cross-Functional Mentor: The Specialist Mentor and Outside Advisor

Symbolized by the key, our Cross-Functional Mentor unlocks doors to realms beyond our immediate function. They broaden our horizons, especially during collaborative endeavors across diverse teams. Their guidance fosters proactive synergy, slashing through silos and paving the way for innovative solutions.

Coach: The Project-Based Tactical Advisor

Echoing the clarion call of the whistle, our Coach infuses our professional journey with purpose and precision. Their laser-focused approach addresses specific challenges, empowering us to tap into and maximize our potential. They may not tread our professional path, but they possess the expertise to guide us through challenges that fall squarely within their wheelhouse.

Sponsor: The Influential Advocate
and Superconnector Advisor

Embodying the essence of a bridge, our Sponsor is our gateway to myriad opportunities within our organization. Their influence is considerable as they connect us to pivotal roles, assignments, and networks, ensuring we traverse the expanse of our potential.

Champion: The Strategic Guide
and "Split-Level" Advisor

Guiding us like a lighthouse amid the extensive professional ocean, our Champion is our beacon of hope and recognition. With a reservoir of experience, often a decade or more than ours, they ensure our contributions don't go unnoticed. They amplify our achievements while ensuring we navigate through challenges and reach the shores of success.

Ally: The Collaborative Partner
and Perspective Advisor

Allies are akin to binoculars. They enhance our worldview, bringing clarity to perspectives and lived experiences outside of our own. They stand with us, not merely as observers but as collaborative partners, enabling us to navigate with confidence and awareness. They don't just understand but actively leverage their privilege to bridge disparities and champion inclusivity. While they may not directly experience the challenges we experience, due to one or more marginalized aspects of our identity, they genuinely commit to understanding and amplifying our voice.

Manager/Supervisor: Your Boss and Daily Advisor

Guiding our professional ship with the precision of a steering wheel, our Managers and Supervisors define our daily course of action. They set clear expectations, provide invaluable feedback, and play a pivotal role in influencing our career trajectory, ensuring our journey is both challenging and rewarding.

Successor: The Protégé-in-Training and Reverse Mentor

Donning the captain's hat in the future, our Successor is an emblem of our legacy. Preparing them to take the helm ensures our endeavors bear fruit even in our absence. This unique relationship is a testament to our dedication to growth, ensuring the vessel of our professional endeavors sails smoothly even after we pass the torch.

Board Seat Matrix Recap

In Part II, we delved deep into engaging with the PBA framework, revealing the intricate roles and attributes that each board member brings to the table. As we wrap up our exploration, it's essential to have a concise summary that can serve as a refresher for your ongoing career journey. Figure 59 provides a snapshot of all PBA seats. (A downloadable copy with even greater detail is available on the companion website.) Remember, while this matrix offers a structured overview, its true potential lies in its adaptability. Your unique career journey might require modifications to this framework. Use the PBA matrix as a foundation, but stay attuned to your needs, challenges, and aspirations. Make the PBA matrix yours, tailor it to your narrative, and set sail toward your professional goals with a well-charted map and a capable crew.

Board Chart	Buddy	Accountability Partner	Functional Mentor	Cross-Functional Mentor	Coach
Seat Details	Peer Support Advisor	Commitment Enforcer and Responsibility Advisor	Experienced Guide and Inside Advisor	Specialist Mentor and Outside Advisor	Project-Based Tactical Advisor
Icon Recap	Life Jacket—keeps you afloat and close in all waters (stormy and calm)	Anchor—keeps you steady, holds you to your word while the swirls of life try to push you around on your journey	Compass—guide you on your path but not directly steering your journey in day-to-day work	Key—open insights to other opportunities and experiences you may not be a part of or aware of	Whistle—call for your attention when needed most and help you focus in near-term on what needs to be worked on
Experience	Within 1–3 Yrs of yours	Within 10 Yrs of yours	Within 5–10 Yrs of yours	Within 5–10 Yrs of yours	Usually at least 10+ Yrs
Internal vs. External	Internal	Likely External, may add Internal Accountability Partner midcareer	Likely Internal for first and second Functional Mentor; may add External Functional Mentor over time	Internal (can be external if you really cannot find one internally)	Usually External (may find internally in larger organizations)
My Goal with Them	Peer support, advice, similar challenges, work-life balance discussion	Accountability, motivation, mental health and emotional well-being, stress management, work-life harmony; focus on defining/refining goals over time and turning them into accomplishments in small steps	Gain insights from their experience, career advice, leadership development, tips on industry trends	Gain knowledge about functions outside of your current role and past experience, exposure to other transferable skills	Gain targeted guidance, develop expertise, enhance focused skill development
Career Map Contributions	Develop first draft and brainstorm "if this, then that" over time	Help you take small steps toward future; ensure they are in alignment with long-term aspirations, prioritize Fun and Personal	Early to mid career—help shape and refine your career map	Map out trajectory aligned with your ambitions, interests, strengths; multiple backup options or pivot opportunities at each future stage	Help achieve near-term accomplishments; may also help with certification milestones
Their Background	Can be similar to yours or vary, important that you get along and they fill most of the "Yes" boxes on the Board Prospect Preparation Checklist from Chapter 3	Can vary, but conversation and feedback style is in strong alignment with yours; helpful to be in similar functions (leadership vs. individual contributor), industry can vary drastically	Similar background and career journey as you, ideally have been in your position before, maybe even worked with your Supervisor before	Different work experience from yours (if you're engineering, they may be marketing, legal, sales, or other non-engineering roles)	Expertise in their field, strong interpersonal skills and communication; background can be different, but must be adept at tailoring coaching to your needs and goals
Meeting Frequency	Daily at start, then weekly and every other week—may be monthly by end of the year	Twice monthly first 2–3 months, then every 4–8 weeks over time	Twice monthly first 3 months, then monthly; maybe 6–8 weeks by end of the year	Twice monthly first 2 months, then every 6–8 weeks through end of the year	Follow guidance; may condense initial frequency, then monthly/every other month

Figure 59: A fully populated PBA Matrix summarizing each of the board seats discussed in Part II, intended as a quick reference guide.

Board Chart	Sponsor	Champion	Ally	Supervisor/ Manager	Successor
Seat Details	Influential Advocate and Superconnector Advisor	Strategic Guide and "Split-Level" Advisor	Collaborative Partner and Perspective Advisor	Your Boss and Daily Advisor	Protege-in-Training and Reverse Mentor
Icon Recap	Bridge—connect to new opportunities and people to cross gaps and stormy waters	Lighthouse—guide from afar, help navigate the long journey, understand larger picture sooner	Binoculars—enhance world view, bring perspective clarity, lived experiences outside of yours	Ship's Helm (steering wheel)—guide daily work; closest to professional development	Captain's Hat—represents passing of the torch and the transition of leadership and responsibility
Experience	10+ Yrs more and one Level above yours	10+ Yrs more and two Levels above yours	Your choice in age and experience	Will vary; don't usually get to choose	5+ Yrs professional in-network (rarely without professional experience)
Internal vs. External	Internal if at all possible	Internal (can be external if you're in a higher level position)	Internal (can be external if you work at a smaller company)	Internal (if entrepreneur, may be filled by other board position)	Internal
My Goal with Them	Amplify your brand and image while not in the room; networking opportunities and introductions	Help understand what is possible; how fit into larger puzzle; more strategic industry trends; promotion strategies	Diversify perspective and inclusivity, how to handle prejudice and discrimination to build bridges together; partner in journey and ensure your path is navigated with wisdom, support, and empathy	Excel in your role, know what is expected, understand performance reviews, goal setting, filling out board with people they suggest	Guide, teach, hand-off role-specific knowledge, skills, and opportunities
Career Map Contributions	Explore opportunities in informational interview (see what may/may not be a good fit)	Work career map backward (begin with the end in mind); understand what can happen at each stage; add details to Achievement column	Review each others' career maps; understand differences in paths taken and plans for future; help each other reach deserved positions	Help understand how current role can build into next; help work on projects and tasks aligned with future roles	Next Steps—how roles contribute to long-term career mapping and the importance of developing pipeline for future success
Their Background	Can vary or be similar; important they have been successful in their professional career	Share your values and care about your career aspirations, have proven track record and strong network; ideally some background and future career map steps overlap	Will come from a different identity group and a stronger position, with influence or power; not under-represented in an area you are	Will vary; don't usually get to choose	Aligned with your recent roles and their future career map roles; focus on completing next future row on their career map
Meeting Frequency	Quarterly; keep cadence throughout career, even if they retire	Every 3–6 months	Monthly	Weekly (live or asynchronous); structure may go to every other week then monthly	Twice monthly to start, will vary over time; monthly structured conversation

In Closing

As we wrap up, thank you for taking the time to read this book and go on this adventure together! I am excited to hear more of your stories and look forward to learning how the PBA + Career Map methodology helps you and the people around you find, build, and sustain growth and success! Remember that the PBA methodology is not a destination but a journey—a dynamic, evolving process tailored to your unique professional path. Revisit this guide regularly, adjust your strategies, realign your board, and, most importantly, continue learning and growing.

SHARE YOUR STORY

I'd love to hear from you! In particular, I would love to hear how the PBA and career map methodology has helped you and the people around you find, build, and sustain growth and success!

Feel free to email (Pathfinders@GoLattitude.com) or if you want a faster reply, complete the "Share Your Story" form on the companion website (QR code on the back of the book or https://www.pathfinders.golattitude.com/book). On social media, use the #PersonalBoardOfAdvisors or #pathfinders hashtags so we can find and reshare your posts. You never know how valuable it can be for someone else to read your story when charting their path.

Get started now!

ACKNOWLEDGMENTS

I am profoundly grateful to the remarkable individuals who have influenced my journey thus far. To those who will undoubtedly join me on this path, I extend my sincere thanks.

This book is dedicated to my immediate family, and I want to express my gratitude once more, extending it to my extended family and friends.

A special thank you to my brother, Luke, who invested endless hours discussing these concepts with me over the past few years.

Jodi D, your unwavering support throughout this project, spanning countless hours, has been indispensable. Without you, this book would not have reached its final form.

To the incredible book writing team, your guidance has been invaluable. Allison, your meticulous editing; Ian, your extensive design expertise; Jodi B, your marketing support and guidance for a first-time author; and Adeline, your final proofreading, have all been instrumental.

A heartfelt thank you to Dr. V for the introduction to this exceptional crew and your invaluable contribution to the Ally chapter.

Danielle and Liv, your dedication during the review and feedback phases, whether at a volleyball game, an event around town, or driving across Pennsylvania, has been deeply appreciated.

Shawn, thank you for your patience during early mornings and late nights, as we refined the core concepts in Part I.

Byron and Melissa, your enduring support and critical feedback on the cover have meant the world to me.

David and Cory, thank you for helping spread the word about this methodology and sharing valuable insights from your journeys.

Frank, you've welcomed me into your world and supported me throughout this book writing and review process, and there's much more to come.

Joe, your mentorship has helped me grow as an entrepreneur, speaker, and author.

Mo, the SEO maestro, and Auggie, our digital media support from afar, your contributions have been remarkable.

To my sister, Kazzy, your motivation, guidance, and unwavering support have been invaluable.

Lastly, a huge thanks to Angelo for taking a leap of faith and joining me on this startup journey. Together, we've recognized the importance of fully developing this book to benefit the world. Let's take the next step of this journey to change more lives, together.

APPENDIX

Companion Website Resources

Access the career map and other PBA resources through the companion website! There you'll find:

1. Career map overview material, pre-mapping exercises, and a brief presentation on the topic
2. Career map worksheets and checklists (blank and samples demonstrating various career stages)
3. Personal Board of Advisors (PBA) overview material, checklists, planning worksheet, and a brief presentation on the topic
4. Personal Board of Advisors (PBA) worksheets (blank and samples demonstrating various career stages)
5. Articles, checklists, infographics, and guides for mentorship and personal development
6. Sample meeting agendas and communication templates (in addition to what was already covered in the book)
7. Suggested calendar/timeline of conversations with your PBA (blank and samples demonstrating various career stages)
8. Glossary of terms and concepts related to advisory relationships
9. Suggested books to read on leadership, self-development, purpose, finding your why, and more
10. Podcasts that align with this book, such as Hidden Brain and On Purpose
11. List of Popular Self-Assessments such as; StrengthsFinder (Now called CliftonStrengths®), Predictive Index® (PI), Emergenetics®, and DiSC® Profile
12. Reach out (by email or the website) to the author of this book, Pete Schramm, as a speaker for your company, association, or school

Suggested Process (with templates from the website):

1. Complete the career map "pre-mapping" planning exercise (ikigai)
2. Complete the first draft of your career map
3. Complete the PBA planning worksheet
4. Develop the first draft of your PBA
5. Review the PBA calendar and edit for your use case
6. Follow the "-iring" process and **get started!**

Made in the USA
Middletown, DE
14 April 2024

52990940R00149